WHAT ARE THEY
TALKING ABOUT?

First published in 2015 by Decani Books, Oak House, 70 High Street, Brandon, Suffolk, IP27 0AU • http://www.decanimusic.co.uk

© 2015 Maurice Taylor

ISBN   978-1-900314-26-8

Printed by Quadrant Design and Print Solutions, Riverside House, Dicker Mill, Hertford, SG13 7AE

What Are They Talking About?

Help for the puzzled and the patient at Sunday Mass

Short background notes for the Collects and the Readings

Maurice Taylor

Decani Books

Acknowledgement

I wish to put on record my gratitude to Nicola Lawrence, a meticulous proof-reader and careful enforcer of uniform consistency of typefaces, spaces and general layout, to Stephen Dean, publisher and constant provider of good advice, and to Fr Philip Kitchen, who took the photograph on the front cover. It shows the attentive congregation at St Margaret's, Ayr, the cathedral church of the diocese of Galloway.

Maurice Taylor, April 2015

Contents

Introduction

There is a problem with Sunday Mass or, to be more specific, with that part of it called the Liturgy of the Word during which we listen to the readings from Scripture. The problem is neither theological nor biblical but rather pastoral or even human.

The Second Vatican Council, in one of its most important documents, The Constitution on the Sacred Liturgy (1963), decreed that

> The treasures of the Bible are to be opened up more lavishly so that a richer fare may be provided for the faithful at the table of God's word. In this way a more representative part of the sacred scriptures will be read to the people in the course of a prescribed number of years (no.51).

Anyone who can remember how the scripture readings at Mass were presented prior to the reforms of Vatican II will be aware how wise and welcome this decree was. In the pre-conciliar Mass, the scripture readings were a truly impoverished part of the liturgy. There was no continuity from day to day or from Sunday to Sunday, there was frequent repetition of a relatively very limited number of passages, the books of the Old Testament were, for all practical purposes, excluded and, whenever the choice of readings was left to the priest, the tendency (to put it no stronger) was to select short and familiar (hackneyed) passages. Attendance at Sunday Mass was an obligation on Catholics but deliberate non-attendance was reckoned only a venial sin as long as one was present for "the Offertory, the Consecration and the Priest's Communion". Hearing the Word of God was not of great importance!

The implementation of the above decree resulted in radical changes to the choice of scripture readings and a greater awareness of the importance of the Liturgy of the Word. The following description of the reforms is limited to the readings chosen for Sunday Masses and those Solemnities and Feasts which, either regularly or occasionally, are celebrated on a Sunday.

We now have three readings on Sundays. Normally, the first of these comes from the Old Testament and, although from Sunday to Sunday there is no sequence or connection between them, each one is deliberately selected for its relation to the gospel passage of the day. However, during the Easter Season (Easter to Pentecost), the first reading comes from the Acts of the Apostles. The theme of the responsorial psalm always has some similarity to the first reading and therefore should allow us some further reflection on it.

The second reading comes from one of the books of the New Testament (apart from the gospels and the Acts of the Apostles). In most cases it is an extract from one of St Paul's letters. The reading appointed for any specific day is not normally related to the first reading or the gospel but the second readings have a sequence in the sense that, over a period of several Sundays, they come from the same book of the New Testament (the letters of Paul, Peter, John or James; and the Apocalypse). On p.22 there is a table showing the selection of second readings on Sundays of Ordinary Time.

During 'Ordinary Time' (that is, excluding Advent and Christmas time and Lent and Easter time, as well as any feasts which displace the Sunday readings), there is a three-year cycle for the synoptic gospels, year A having extracts from Matthew's account of Christ's public ministry, year B and year C being devoted to Mark's and Luke's gospels respectively. There are a few exceptions to this arrangement, the most notable being in year B when, for five Sundays (from Sundays 17 to 21 in Ordinary Time) Mark's gospel is interrupted and John's gospel, chapter 6, is inserted instead. John's gospel is also frequently used on the Sundays of Lent and Easter time, while during the Christmas season the 'infancy gospels' of Matthew and Luke are prominent.

All of that is fairly complicated but fortunately the correct choices are laid out for us in the lectionary. So my laboured explanation (which has omitted some of the exceptions) is merely for information. The point I want to make is on the subject of the scripture readings but not on the actual selections which have been set out for us.

Rather, my point is the following. The readings are meant to be read well and to be heard by us. And the aim is that we should be able to take in what we hear, to retain at least something, to consider and reflect on it and to be affected by it. But conditions and circumstances seem to make that almost impossible to achieve. The needs of the situation at Mass seem to dictate that the readings are delivered one after another, with little or no time for silences between the readings. Even if the readers are excellent and completely audible, it is just not humanly possible for us to retain more than a few bits and pieces of what we hear. Just think of it! Old Testament reading, responsorial psalm (and the response to be remembered), New Testament reading, gospel acclamation, and gospel passage – and all immediately preceded by the Collect, the opening prayer, 'through which the character of the celebration finds expression' (as the official description unrealistically puts it). That makes a total of six very different passages presented to us one after another and with, at best, minimal pauses between each of them. Is it any wonder that we feel frustrated – or just numb?

Can anything be done, if not to rectify matters at least to ameliorate the situation?

Fewer readings? That would mean abandoning the Old Testament, or St Paul, or the psalms.

Longer pauses? That would take courage (or unreal expectations) on the part of the priest or the parish liturgy committee. "The people like quick Masses."

Serious preparation on the part of those intending to participate in Mass? Yes, but...

So the purpose of this book is to offer ordinary people the opportunity to anticipate what they are going to hear in the Collect and the scripture readings on any given Sunday. It is not primarily for priests (unless they want to use it) and it is definitely not hints for homilists. My hope is simply this: that those who would like to have some idea of what they are going to hear at Mass will read the appropriate notes for the Sunday, hoping that, with that modest preparation, they will be enabled to listen with more understanding and retain more easily some of the 'richer fare' provided for us at 'the table of God's word'. The prayer in the Divine Office will then seem more authentic: "Praise to you, Lord God, for the table of your word to bring us light and joy".

The Old Testament
Some additional helpful notes

The Old Testament is the usual name that Christians give to the Jewish Scriptures. They comprise all the various books that treat of God's relationship with the human race from creation until the time of Jesus. Christians see in them frequent references to the coming of a messiah – a messiah whom we recognise in Jesus Christ.

The various books of the Old Testament are usually divided into three categories: historical books, prophets and wisdom books. Let us briefly consider each category.

Historical Books

The Pentateuch

The first five books in this category are known as the Pentateuch (a word derived from Greek and meaning five volumes). They are also known collectively as the Torah ('the Law'). They are Genesis, Exodus, Leviticus, Numbers and Deuteronomy.

Genesis Chapters 1 to 11 contain some historical traces but their primary purpose is to provide religious teaching. They tell of the goodness of the creator God and of the plight of the human race, created in the image of God yet distant from God through sin. From chapters 12 to 50 we are told about the ancient ancestors of the Jewish people, starting with Abraham and continuing through Isaac, Jacob, his twelve sons (from whom come the Twelve Tribes of Israel) and with special emphasis on Joseph.

Exodus describes the escape of the chosen people, led by Moses, from slavery in Egypt, their journey through the wilderness and God's revelation at Mount Sinai to Moses, revealing his august name, his covenant with the Jews, and his laws for them.

Leviticus is taken up with further laws and ordinances for the people.

Numbers resumes the account of the Israelites' journey through the desert.

Deuteronomy comprises discourses of Moses (largely taken up with recalling events during and following the escape from Egypt), more religious and civil laws (some repeated from earlier decrees) and the death of Moses at the end of the journey.

Scripture scholars tell us that the material in the Pentateuch comes from various ancient sources and that, later on, different elements from these sources were assembled into four separate traditions, called Yahwist (from its use of the word *Yahweh* for God), Elohist (which, for God, uses *Elohim*), Deuteronomic and Priestly. These traditions or 'codes', existing side by side in the Pentateuch, mean that there is frequent duplication. The most obvious example of this is the two accounts of creation in the Book of Genesis: the Priestly narrative (1:1-2:4) and the Yahwist narrative (2:5-25). The first is theological, abstract, orderly, schematic, with God a transcendent kingly creator; the second is more lively and colourful, with dialogue and anthropomorphisms, and with man as its centre of interest.

Later history

Joshua and Judges. Subsequent historical books of the Old Testament continue directly from Deuteronomy (at whose conclusion Moses appoints Joshua as his successor and then dies). The book of **Joshua** narrates how Joshua led the chosen people across the Jordan into the Promised Land, conquered it and assigned territory to each of the twelve tribes. The book of **Judges** deals with those who governed Israel after the death of Joshua – not kings since, at the time, the belief prevailed that only God could be their king. The book of Judges also describes the wars which were fought, not only against the Canaanites (whom the Israelites had expelled) but also against neighbouring peoples (Moabites, Philistines and others).

1040 - 931 BC

The kings - Saul, David, Solomon. The books of **Samuel** **(I & II)** and **Kings (I & II)** tell first of events from 1040 to 931 BC: Samuel, the last of the judges; Saul, the first of the kings, rejected in favour of David, who is succeeded by his son Solomon, builder of the first temple.

Conflict and exile

Two kingdoms. At the death of Solomon, the kingdom of Israel split into two separate and mutually unfriendly kingdoms: Judah in the south (the tribes of Judah and Simeon, with the city of Jerusalem) and Israel in the north (the other ten tribes). The history of the two kingdoms is, on the whole, a dismal one. Religious schism in the northern kingdom, strife between the two kingdoms, attacks from other nations, immoral and inadequate rulers (most of them, not all) and, in general, declining standards of worship, morality and prosperity.

To the east of Palestine (roughly, in present day Iraq), three pagan nations (Assyrians, Chaldeans and Babylonians) were engaged in wars against one another and, at various times, one or other of the three emerged stronger than the others. During much of the eighth and seventh centuries BC, Assyria (especially under King Sennacherib) was dominant; in the sixth century, it was the Chaldeans (especially during the long reign of King Nebuchadnezzar). In the wars of the time, the city of Babylon was the prize that whichever kingdom was dominant at any time sought to win and occupy.

The northern kingdom conquered. Nevertheless, the two Jewish kingdoms also attracted the hostile attention of the pagan kingdoms. In 734 BC half of the northern kingdom of Israel was incorporated into Assyria and in 721 BC Assyria conquered the remainder of Israel and deported many of the inhabitants to a number of places then under Assyrian domination. The result of this widespread dispersal and, at the same time, the arrival in Samaria (the greater part of the northern kingdom) of many Assyrians who incorporated Jewish beliefs and practices into their pagan religion, meant that the northern kingdom of Israel never recovered its authentic Jewish identity. Instead, Samaria was seen by genuine Jews as a heretic and hostile land while the dispersal, absorption and disappearance of the northern tribes fostered the legend of "the lost tribes of Israel".

734, 721 BC

The southern kingdom conquered - the Babylonian exile. The threat of the Assyrians for the rest of Palestine diminished, but the Chaldeans under King Nebuchadnezzar became an even greater danger. Some Jews (including the prophet Daniel and his three young companions) had been deported to Babylon in 605 BC. The Chaldeans invaded Judah in 598, captured Jerusalem and deported more of the citizens to Babylon. In 587, they again invaded, destroyed the city and the temple and carried out a third deportation.

587 BC

Return from exile - Persian rule. The Chaldean practice was to deport the leading and prominent citizens, the educated and the affluent. However, in 539 Babylon fell to the Persian armies under Cyrus who, with an edict the following year, allowed the return of the exiled Jews to Palestine. On returning to Jerusalem the Jews immediately began work on the second temple which was dedicated in 515 BC (and remained until 19 BC when Herod the Great began his project of replacing it with a much grander construction).

Greek rule. The period of Persian hegemony ended in 331 BC with the victory of Alexander the Great and the start of the hellenistic period which was to last until 63 BC. During this time the Seleucid dynasty (named after its founder Seleucus I) was the most important power and, at its height, their rule extended from the Aegean to the Indus. Palestine

331-63 BC

was subject to considerable hellenisation with Greek culture, language and customs becoming widespread. The Hebrew Bible was translated into Greek (called the 'Septuagint' because there were seventy translators) but, from 167 to 164 BC, a very severe persecution occurred when those Jews who resisted attempts to abolish Jewish worship and substitute worship of Zeus in the temple were subjected to a reign of terror.

Roman rule. In 64 BC at Antioch in Syria, the Roman general Pompey **63 BC-36 AD** deposed the last of the Seleucid rulers. Pompey captured Jerusalem the following year and Palestine passed into Roman occupation. Local rulers were appointed by the emperor in Rome, Herod the Great being king from 37 to 4 BC. Jesus was born between 8 and 4 BC, probably 7-6. Herod Antipas, son of Herod the Great, was tetrarch (= ruler of the fourth part of a region or, in general, a satellite prince) of Galilee (4BC-39AD). Pontius Pilate was governor/procurator of Judaea (and Samaria) (26-36AD).

The Prophets

The prophets of Israel have immediate experience of God, whose holiness and will are revealed to them. They see the present and the future through God's eyes and are sent to remind us of our duty to God and to bring us back to obedience and love. They are providential instruments of God for the guidance of his people.

Moses is the first and greatest, but he was followed by many others: Joshua, Deborah, Samuel, Nathan, Elijah, Elisha and others (late 13th to early 8th centuries BC). More explicitly, we consider the prophets who have left us their written testimonies. The great era of these writer-prophets is from mid-eighth to mid-sixth century BC (at the end of the exile). The three most common and important themes on which they prophesied to the people can be stated as follows:

• *Monotheism* (there is one and only one God, transcendent, holy, mysterious, yet near us, to be praised and thanked);

• *Morality* (it is our sinfulness that separates us from God; sin deserves punishment by God, but God is infinitely merciful); and

• *Messianic Hope* (God will send us a Saviour who will lead us into true and perfect happiness in his kingdom; on earth, the messiah, anointed to royal dignity, will be God's representative).

Among the prophets whose teachings have been collected, there are four called 'major' because of the length of their writings, and twelve 'minor' prophets.

The four major prophets are Isaiah, Jeremiah, Ezekiel and Daniel. The twelve minor prophets are Hosea, Joel, Amos, Obadiah, Jonah, Micah, Nahum, Habakkuk, Zephaniah, Haggai, Zechariah and Malachi.

Isaiah

The writings of Isaiah are divided into three parts, known as First Isaiah (chapters 1-39), Second Isaiah (40-55) and Third Isaiah (56-66) because the first and second sections (the latter often called Deutero-Isaiah) come from the eighth and sixth centuries BC respectively. Deutero-Isaiah seems to have been the work of a follower of Isaiah but of unknown identity. The third section's source is uncertain but it may be a sequel added to the second.

Isaiah ('First Isaiah') received his call from God in 740 BC and he proclaims the fall of both Israel and Judah because of their infidelity. The two kingdoms, especially Judah, began making treaties with some of the neighbouring countries and against others. Isaiah pleaded that it was not such treaties that should be the policy, but trust in God. The fate of both kingdoms continued on the road to ruin with exile for many of the people.

Isaiah became a national figure. He was a fine poet but, above all, his outstanding gift was in his religious faith – his desire to proclaim the oneness, the transcendence and the justice of God; his awareness of our sinfulness yet his certainty that salvation will come with the coming of the messiah.

In Second Isaiah, the people are in exile in Babylon but with hopes of being able to return to their homeland (an event which actually took place in 538 BC). The book contains the four 'songs of the servant of the Lord', prophecies about a perfect disciple of God who will suffer to atone for the sins of the people but who, in the end, will be exalted by God. These 'songs' are, of course, clearly messianic and are very prominent on various occasions in the Liturgy of the Word, especially in Holy Week.

Jeremiah

Jeremiah was born near Jerusalem and began his work in 626 BC. He passed his life through the years leading up to the ruin of the kingdom of Judah, brought on by attempts to counter the increasing strength and menace of the Chaldeans. Judah rebelled, was besieged and captured and eventually (587) the city and temple were destroyed, many of the inhabitants being deported to Babylon. Jeremiah tirelessly preached, prophesied disaster, warned the kings, pleaded with the people through all the disasters. He remained in Jerusalem until taken to Egypt where he died. In his character, Jeremiah was an admirable man, gentle and kind, devout and committed. Despite his nature, his sense of duty meant that he was constantly condemning kings, priests, false prophets, the nation itself. The climax of his work is in his prophecy of the new covenant to be achieved in messianic times (31:31-34).

Two short books, Lamentations and Baruch, are usually attributed to close followers or disciples of Jeremiah.

Ezekiel

Ezekiel is a contemporary of Jeremiah but probably carried out his work while in exile in Babylon (593-571). He reproaches the people still in Jerusalem as well as the nations who had influenced the Israelites; then he consoles his people during and after the siege, assuring them of a better future and indicating the need for political and religious change when the exiles will have returned to Palestine.

Ezekiel was a priest and shows special concern for the temple and the Law. He uses symbolic gestures and he recounts four visions which he has experienced, couched in language of fantasy (as, for example, the animals of the Lord's chariot (1:4-12), the dry bones that come to life (37:1-14), the future temple with the river flowing through it (47:1-12). His messiah will be a shepherd rather than a glorious king and he uses the term 'son of man' which Daniel reworked and Jesus adopted to refer to himself.

Daniel

The book of Daniel is a much later production than the other three major prophets. It was written during a severe persecution of the Jews from 167 to 164 BC. However, the subject matter belongs to the era of the Babylonian exile – Daniel's exploits in the service of Nebuchadnezzar and his successors, followed by Daniel's visions during the reigns of the great king's successors and of Cyrus king of Persia The aim of the book is to encourage the Jews during the later persecution since Daniel and his companions had been victorious after similar ordeals. The end will come, the suffering will cease and the everlasting kingdom will be established, ruled by the 'son of man' (7:13). (Ezekiel had used this term but without the eschatalogical connotation that Daniel gives it.) The theme of the coming of the kingdom is prevalent throughout the book and reappears as the central theme of the synoptic gospels. Jesus calls himself 'Son of Man' to declare that he is the fulfilment of the prophecies of Daniel.

The Minor Prophets

The Minor Prophets are used less frequently in the Liturgy of the Word. Brief details of their lives and work will be given as their writings occur and if details are known.

The following is a chronological list:-

14

Amos (783-743), born in Judah, shepherd, a prophet to the northern kingdom of Israel

Hosea (c.783-after 743), native of and prophet to the northern kingdom of Israel

Micah (between 750 and 687) from near Hebron, a prophet to Judah

Zephaniah (after 640-?), a prophet to Judah

Nahum (before 612-?), a prophet...; exulted at the fall of Nineveh and Assyria (612)

Habakkuk (active c.600), a prophet...; he and Nahum are contemporary with Jeremiah

Haggai (active 520), first post-exilic prophet

Zechariah (520-518) and **Deutero-Zechariah** (end of 4th century), details unknown

Malachi (after 516 but before 445), details unknown

Obadiah (before 312), identity and details of author unknown

Joel (c.400), no further details known

Jonah (probably 5th century), a droll and fictitious story to amuse and instruct

The Wisdom Books

The Wisdom Books of the Old Testament are **Job, Proverbs, Ecclesiastes, Song of Songs, Ecclesiasticus** and **Wisdom**. Writings on the subject of Wisdom were common throughout the civilisations of the East in Old Testament times. They dealt with issues and problems concerned with human beings, although the approach was not philosophical (as was the basis of Greek thought) but came rather from experience and was devoted to the destiny of the individual. The earliest works of Israel were concerned with similar themes but gradually religion began to play a part in the works on Wisdom by Jewish writers. Hence the contrast between wisdom and folly developed into the difference between virtue and vice, between true and false religion. The Jewish sages realised that all Wisdom comes from God and that our final destiny depends on God and is therefore a matter for reward or punishment. They were concerned with the lives and conduct of individuals and, in this, are different from the prophets and their preaching and writing.

The Psalms are sometimes included among the Wisdom Books. It seems preferable to consider them separately.

The Book of Job has been called 'the literary masterpiece of the wisdom movement'. As a framework for his story, the author uses the tradition of a famous man, wise and God-fearing, who lived many centuries earlier. The identity of the author is unknown. He was Jewish, probably lived in Palestine and probably in post-exilic times, perhaps in early fifth century BC. The book is the story of a good man who suffers. His friends conclude that suffering is the consequence of sin, which Job cannot accept. He appeals to God who will say only that his divine actions and plans are inscrutable. At that stage of revelation, the author could go no further. The lesson of the story is that faith must remain even when our understanding does not offer an explanation.

The Book of Proverbs begins with a long prologue in which a father commends wisdom to his son (1:8-9:18) and it ends with an epilogue which is a poem about the ideal wife, the verses beginning with successive letters of the Hebrew alphabet (31:10-31). Between these two, there are the proverbs or aphorisms or maxims. The earliest chapters (10-22 & 25-29) probably date from the time of Solomon (tenth century).

Ecclesiastes (or 'Qoheleth' = president or spokesman of the public assembly) is attributed to Solomon (but this is only a convention to recommend the work, which is post-exilic). The theme is the emptiness of all apparently good things, whether wealth, knowledge, love or life itself. We must accept whatever sorrows and joys God sends and, without God needing to explain his actions or treatment of us, we must obey.

The Song of Songs is a collection of love poems of post-exilic times. There are two common interpretations of the book. First, the literal interpretation of poems about true human love, sanctified by union; second, the allegorical interpretation expressed as the love between God and Israel or Christ and the Church or God and the individual soul.

Ecclesiasticus (or 'Sirach') dates from early in the second century BC. The rule of the Seleucids had just begun in Palestine and the book urges the Jews to remain faithful to their religion and worship and to God's commandments and not to become infected with the Seleucid Greek pagan beliefs and practices. The author, Ben Sira, then offers to teach wisdom and does so with maxims on a wide variety of subjects. His understanding of wisdom is bound up with observance of the Law given by God to Moses and with the performance of religious duties. He reflects on the history of salvation but has little to say about hope of a messiah.

The Book of Wisdom, originally in Greek, was written by a Jew living in Alexandria in mid-first century BC. Its main purpose is to dissuade Jews from being wooed from their faith and practices by the attractions of Greek cultural life in Alexandria (philosophy, physical sciences, mystery religions and beliefs).

The author commends wisdom which is sought by prayer to God and is the source of all virtue. He goes further than earlier Jewish sages and solves the problem of retribution by distinguishing body from soul so that this life is a preparation for eternal life in which the good are with God and the wicked are punished. Though the author associates wisdom closely with God, he does make a distinction between them if not a separate existence (7:22-8:8); and this advance in thinking is used in the New Testament theology on the Word of God (especially John 1:1-5 & 9-14; 3:16-17; 5:20).

The Psalms

Poetry was very popular throughout the Middle East and from the earliest times. Most of the religious poetry of Israel is preserved in the 150 psalms of the Psalter. The psalms can be divided into three literary types: hymns of praise; psalms of entreaty, both collective and individual; psalms of thanksgiving. This division is not precise since there are many psalms of composite types. The Psalter is Israel's hymn book; the temple had, and synagogues have, their cantors. The psalms were related to public worship though in only a few cases is the particular occasion known for which a psalm was composed or on which a psalm would have been sung.

Many thought that King David was the author of all the psalms, but this view is very unlikely. It seems certain that he composed some, but we do not know which or how many. (Inscribing a psalm to David is not a proof of authorship; it may mean only 'dedicated to' or an enthusiastic exaggeration.) Some psalms come from the time of the kings, some from during the exile, some are post-exilic (when the temple was rebuilt and public worship was renewed); there may even be some from the Seleucid hellenistic period (after 300 BC) – psalms 44(45), 74(75), 79(80) and 83(84) have been suggested.

Jesus, Mary and the apostles all prayed the psalms. We still use them unchanged as official prayers. Their praise, entreaty and thanksgiving have universal relevance but with greatly enhanced significance for Christians. We know more of the love of God, the tragedy of sin, the promise of glory. The hopes of the psalmists have been realised, the messiah has come, we are invited to worship in the kingdom he inaugurated.

The New Testament

A few points that are relevant and of interest

The Synoptic Problem

The fact that there is an obvious similarity in the content and even in the wording of the gospels of Matthew, Mark and Luke has led to them being called the synoptics (a word which might be rendered as 'lookalikes'). The problem is to find the reason for this strange mixture of similar and dissimilar material in the three gospels.

Before outlining some attempts to explain the similarities, here are some dissimilarities. First, Matthew and Luke give accounts of the infancy of Jesus, but Mark does not; besides, the accounts of the infancy given by Matthew and Luke differ considerably between them. Second, the three temptations of Jesus are reported by Matthew and Luke (but the order is changed) but Mark gives no details at all. Third, the reports of Christ's trial, passion and death differ in the three gospels. Fourth, the details of the resurrection and post-resurrection appearances are even more varied.

There is further general dissimilarity in the reporting of Jesus' discourses and sayings.

In this, Mark's material is sparse, Matthew's and Luke's much more abundant but, whereas in Matthew, the material is placed in five great discourses of Jesus, in Luke it is presented as being said during a long journey to Jerusalem. Finally, to give a couple of more familiar examples of diversity, Matthew has eight beatitudes, Luke only four; Matthew's 'Our Father' has seven petitions, Luke's only five.

So how did the three gospels, with their similarities but also their differences, come to be? It is agreed by most scholars that there was an existing oral tradition, dating from the time of Jesus himself. There is also general agreement that Mark (in Greek) is the earliest written gospel (probably 65-70 AD) and that it is a source for Matthew and Luke. The rest of the material in Matthew and Luke would seem to require other source(s) and it is conjectured that, where the two gospels have the same non-Mark material, it came from a now unknown document (called by scholars 'Q'); and that, where either has material not in the other, it came from now unidentified sources. The dates when Matthew and Luke were written can only be conjectured. Most suggest some time after 70 AD.

The Gospel of St John

It is reasonable to assume that the fourth gospel is the work of John, the apostle and the son of Zebedee, although he may have been helped by a disciple-scribe. Further, the date of writing would seem to have been towards the end of the first century. In fact, the fourth gospel is very different from the other three in content, style and wording, as the following indications make clear.

First, its opening chapter, called the Prologue, presents Jesus as the Word of God who was always with God and is indeed himself God and who became a human being, 'sent' to be our Saviour. His disciples 'see his glory' from the start and, throughout the gospel, Jesus is acclaimed as messiah. The more gradual development of Jesus' messianic proclamation, as described in the synoptics, is more in conformity with the manner in which the disciples came to know of it. John's method, and particularly his identifying Jesus not only as the Son of God but also as the Word, seems to be the culmination of the Old Testament's gradual development of thought about Wisdom and its relationship to God.

Second, the miracles of Jesus are presented as signs, not so much to announce the kingdom but rather to reveal the full identity of Jesus. Cana, Nicodemus, the Samaritan woman, the man born blind, Lazarus – all help us to recognise Jesus and to enrich our faith in him. In particular, several times in these stories and elsewhere, Jesus employs the phrase 'I am' to introduce a description of himself and his mission (for example, 9:5, 10:11, 11:25 and 15:1).

Third, the synoptics treat of Christ's 'coming' and glorification as to be expected at the end of time. In John's gospel, however, the 'coming' is interpreted as happening at the incarnation and crucifixion. Consequently, judgment occurs in this life (3:18), eternal life is received through faith (5:24) and Jesus is the resurrection and life now for those who believe (11:25).

Fourth, the synoptic gospels do not speak of any early association of some of the disciples of Christ with John the Baptist (as the fourth gospel does) and they limit Jesus' public ministry in Jerusalem to one single visit there while the fourth gospel reports several visits to the city. In both of these cases, John's version seems more likely.

Fifth, the manner in which John narrates the last supper, the passion and death of Jesus and his resurrection and subsequent appearances is very different from the synoptics' accounts. The fourth gospel alone tells us that, at the supper, Jesus washed the feet of the disciples. It does not mention the consecration of the bread and wine for eucharistic communion, but it presents an extended discourse to the disciples and a long prayer to the Father on the subjects of unity and love and with a number of references to the coming of the Holy Spirit, the Advocate, to us, the Church. Then, the passion and death of Jesus are, as already mentioned, reported in terms of the glorification of Jesus, who is composed and courageous throughout. The agony of Jesus in the garden is omitted, he remains in control as he encounters those sent to arrest him as well as those who question him on trial. Only John reports the outcome of the dispute about the inscription on the cross and he alone mentions the presence of Mary on Calvary.

The resurrection and the appearances that followed continue to show the victorious Christ and they culminate, at the end of chapter 20, with Thomas's acclamation, 'My Lord and my God', the fullest and most complete declaration of Christ's identity made by anyone in the gospels. It echoes the opening words of the fourth gospel ('...the Word was God') and is the act of faith of all of us, disciples of Jesus Christ.

That is how John ends his gospel. Subsequently, chapter 21 was added, either by John or by others, to record evidence of other and very significant actions of the risen Lord.

The fourth gospel, coming from a different tradition than the synoptics' sources (of which, in all probability John was aware), undoubtedly adds to our knowledge of Jesus and his ministry. But the purpose of John's gospel is not to relate events as they would be seen by a detached and neutral reporter but, rather, to tell the story faithfully (the Christ of history) but also to bring out their meaning as signs, to show that they are divine as well as human signs of what Christ brought to the world – new life, purification, living water, living bread, light.

St Paul

• His Travels

The First Missionary Journey (with Barnabas as companion) was from AD 46 to 49. Its route was from Antioch in Syria to Cyprus, then to Asia Minor on the coast (Perga) and various towns inland (Pisidian Antioch, Iconium, Lystra and Derbe), before returning to Syrian Antioch.

The Second Missionary Journey (with Silas and, later, Timothy and Luke as companions) was from AD 49 to 52. Its route went overland to Asia Minor (Derbe and Lystra), through Phrygia to northern Galatia and on to Troas; then by sea to Greece (Philippi, Thessalonika, Athens, and 18 months at Corinth); finally by sea to Ephesus and Caesarea Maritima.

The Third Missionary Journey was from AD 54 to 57. The route was overland through northern Galatia and Phrygia to Ephesus (three years there including a short visit to Corinth), from Ephesus to Macedonia and Corinth (three months) back to Macedonia (at Philippi), then by ship, visiting many coastal towns in Asia Minor and islands in the Aegean, to Caesarea Maritima and on to Jerusalem (at Pentecost AD 58).

Paul's final known journey was as a prisoner from Jerusalem (AD 58) to Caesarea Maritima (two years in prison), by sea (AD 60 autumn) by Asia Minor (Myra and Cnidus) and Crete to Malta (shipwrecked, AD 60-61 winter), by ship via Siracusa and Reggio di Calabria to Puteoli and then overland, to Rome (AD 61 spring) and house arrest (AD 61 to 63). Thereafter, details are unknown. Was Paul set free from house arrest in AD 63 for more travel (Asia Minor, Macedonia and Greece) before further imprisonment in Rome and martyrdom?

• His Letters

AD 51 (early months)	I and II Thessalonians (sent from Corinth)
c. 54	Galatians (sent from Ephesus)
c. 56	Philippians (sent from Ephesus)
57 (Pentecost)	I Corinthians (sent from Ephesus)
57 (autumn)	II Corinthians (sent from Macedonia)
58 (early months)	Romans (sent from Corinth)
61-63	Ephesians (sent from Rome)
61-63	Colossians (sent from Rome)
61-63	Philemon (sent from Rome)
c. 65	I Timothy (sent from Macedonia)
c. 65	Titus (sent from Macedonia)
c. 67	II Timothy (sent from Rome)

Many scholars have raised doubts concerning the authorship (and dates) of several of the letters, especially those to the Ephesians, the Colossians, Timothy and Titus. From internal evidence, it is argued that they may have been written by a secretary at Paul's behest or by a later follower of Paul wishing to develop the apostle's thinking.

To complete the dating of the Second Readings:-

AD 45-62? Letter of James (not an apostle; 'the brother of the Lord'?)

AD 63-70? Letter to the Hebrews (author unknown)

Sunday Second Readings (Ordinary Time)

Sunday	Year A	Year B	Year C
2	I Corinthians 1-4	I Corinthians 6-11	I Corinthians 12-15
3	"	"	"
4	"	"	"
5	"	"	"
6	"	"	"
7	"	II Corinthians	"
8	"	"	"
9	Romans	"	Galatians
10	"	"	"
11	"	"	"
12	"	"	"
13	"	"	"
14	"	"	"
15	"	Ephesians	Colossians
16	"	"	"
17	"	"	"
18	"	"	"
19	"	"	Hebrews 11-12
20	"	"	"
21	"	"	"
22	"	James	"
23	"	"	Philemon
24	"	"	I Timothy
25	Philippians	"	"
26	"	"	"
27	"	Hebrews 2-10	II Timothy
28	"	"	"
29	I Thessalonians	"	"
30	"	"	"
31	"	"	II Thessalonians
32	"	"	"
33	"	"	"

The Sunday Collects and Readings of Year A

Advent and Christmas, Year A

The First Sunday of Advent • Year A

*'Advent' means 'coming' and therefore, for us, it involves a time of 'waiting'.
But this should be understood as having a sense of 'desire' and 'expectancy'.*

Collect

We pray that we may meet Jesus when he comes and that he will take us into the Kingdom of God.

First Reading   Isaiah 2:1-5

The prophet Isaiah, writing in the 730s BC, looks forward to a day when Judah and Jerusalem will be so famous that all nations, 'peoples without number', will go there to learn the teaching of their God and follow his ways of peace. The Church sees this prophecy as looking forward to messianic times.

Psalm 121 (122)

*I rejoiced when I heard them say:
'Let us go to God's house'.*

The pilgrim's joy on the way to Jerusalem (which may be understood as also the heavenly Jerusalem).

Second Reading   Romans 13:11-14

From St Paul to the Romans (also on Sundays 2 & 4). The night is almost over, the daylight of salvation is at hand; so let us live decently. The comments (below) on the gospel for today are also relevant for this reading.

Gospel   Matthew 24:37-44

Today we begin Year A, the 'Year of Matthew'.

In Matthew's gospel, chapter 24, Jesus says that we shall not receive a warning that the Son of Man is about to appear; so be prepared. The early Christians at first expected Christ's second coming imminently and, when it did not occur, they had to be kept alert. So have we. Although the passage refers primarily to the second coming, it also reminds us of the Saviour's birth at Bethlehem – and indeed of the coming judgment for each one of us.

The Second Sunday of Advent • Year A

Advent is a time of waiting, but our waiting should be a 'looking forward' with joy and hope. Today's liturgy is about the coming of Christ, the Messiah, but not specifically about his birth at Bethlehem.

Collect

May God help us to be anxious to meet his Son and to have the faith we need in order to be in his company.

First Reading   Isaiah 11:1-10

From the prophecy of Isaiah. This magnificent passage is a messianic poem about the coming of a king who will bring salvation and peace for all.

Note the words: 'On him the spirit of the Lord rests', followed by a list of the qualities to be conferred on this person: wisdom, insight, counsel, power, knowledge, fear of the Lord. These (with piety, found in some texts but synonymous with fear of the Lord) become the Christian 'seven gifts of the Holy Spirit'. References to the spirit (= breath) of the Lord are found throughout the Old Testament and reach their perfect fulfilment in the Person of the Holy Spirit, revealed in the New Testament and in the early Church.

Psalm 71(72)

> *In his days justice shall flourish*
> *and peace till the moon fails.*

The psalm was composed as a tribute to and a prayer for King Solomon, son of David. Both Jewish and Christian traditions interpret it as also referring to the king foreseen by Isaiah in the passage used as today's first reading.

Second Reading   Romans 15:4-9

St Paul, in this extract from his letter to the Christians in Rome, appeals to them (and to us all) to be united in hope, tolerant and friendly to one another, and aware that God's mercy is for all, gentiles as well as Jews.

Gospel   Matthew 3:1-12

St Matthew's gospel describes John the Baptist, precursor and herald of Christ. In a severe criticism of some religious leaders, John contrasts himself with Jesus and declares the latter's superiority. John's baptism is with water and only for repentance; Christ's will be with the Holy Spirit and with fire, this latter seen as a symbol of purification.

The Third Sunday of Advent • Year A

'Are you the one for whom we are waiting?' This question is still being asked today.

Collect

Looking forward to the feast of Christ's Nativity, we ask God to enable us to obtain the salvation that Jesus brings and to celebrate that grace with true joy.

First Reading
Isaiah 35:1-6.10

Today's reading from Isaiah (or perhaps Second Isaiah) was a poem composed to celebrate God's love in bringing his people back from exile. In the liturgy, we use the passage to celebrate God's salvation of us through the coming of his Son.

Psalm 145 (146)

Come, Lord, and save us.

A prayer of praise and thanksgiving to God for his loving care. It forms part of the morning prayer of religious Jews.

Second Reading
James 5:7-10

From the letter of James, known as 'the brother of the Lord' although in all probability not one of the Twelve.

The extract counsels patience in waiting for the Lord (specifically, in the letter, the second coming of Christ) and urges Christians to treat each other with kindness.

Gospel
Matthew 11:2-11

In today's passage from St Matthew's gospel, John the Baptist is in prison and has heard of Jesus and his public ministry. He is surprised that the ministry is so gentle and caring and without violent condemnations. So is he truly the messiah or, like John himself, a precursor? Jesus reassures his cousin and then speaks highly of him to the people. The incident is relevant for Advent, but only rather obliquely.

The Fourth Sunday of Advent • Year A

With the feast of Christmas now only days away, today's Mass and especially the readings concentrate only on the first coming of the Lord.

Collect

This prayer, already well known to many of us, expresses our awareness of Our Lord's coming among us as man and asks God for the grace that, through his Son's passion and death, we may share in his resurrection.

First Reading   Isaiah 7:10-14

This famous passage in Isaiah is directly a prophecy to reassure King Ahaz of Judah (late 8th century BC) as he dreaded an end to his reign and to his Davidic dynasty. But from the start, Christians have seen the words as a hidden prophecy of the birth of Jesus, the awaited messiah. This is particularly because of the name to be given to the child ('Immanuel') and the use of the word for the child's mother: 'a young (recently married) woman' in the Hebrew text, but 'a virgin' in the Greek text.

Psalm 23 (24)

Let the Lord enter!
He is the king of glory.

The psalm speaks of God's desire to be close to those who seek him with sincerity.

Second Reading   Romans 1:1-7

This reading is the opening of St Paul's letter to the Christians of Rome. He introduces his theme: the Son of God, through whom Paul received his mission to preach the gospel of salvation to all nations.

Gospel   Matthew 1:18-24

St Matthew recounts the events which affected Mary and Joseph before the birth of their son. It is important to note the prominence given to the names of their son: 'Jesus' which means 'Saviour' (and who comes in humility and poverty, not in grandeur or power) and 'Emmanuel' which means 'God is with us' (recalling today's first reading and, though descriptive rather than the given name, an astonishing claim that demands a response of faith).

The Nativity of the Lord • Years A,B,C
(Mass during the night)

Collect

In the light of this unique night, we pray that we who know the truth of this light on earth will enjoy its eternal splendour in heaven.

First Reading   Isaiah 9:1-7

This passage by the prophet Isaiah, written in the late 8th century BC when Jews of the northern Israel kingdom were being deported by the Assyrians, looks forward to the people's return to their homeland in peaceful times. The application of it to the birth of Jesus is traditional and evident.

Psalm 95 (96)

Today a saviour has been born to us;
he is Christ the Lord.

This psalm is a hymn of joy, celebrating the coming of God, a just ruler, to our world.

Second Reading   Titus 2:11-14

St Paul, in the letter to Titus, his former pupil and now in charge of the Christians in Crete, reminds us that the presence on earth of God's divine Son and our Saviour calls us to live in a new and moral manner.

Gospel   Luke 2:1-14

The Midnight Mass gospel is St Luke's account of the birth of Jesus.

Not only the date but even the actual year of Christ's birth in unknown. It must have been before the death in 4 BC of Herod the Great; so probably between 8 and 4 BC.

The angel speaks of Christ as 'the Lord', a title in the Old Testament reserved for God.

The Nativity of the Lord • Years A,B,C
(Mass at dawn)

Collect

The birth of Jesus brings a new light to the world. May the light of faith shine out in our lives.

First Reading   Isaiah 62:11-12

This reading from Isaiah, originally composed (probably in the sixth century BC) to celebrate the return of the Jews from exile in Babylon and a glorious restoration of the city of Jerusalem, is now applied to the birth of Christ.

Psalm 96 (97)

This day new light will shine upon the earth: the Lord is born for us.

Today we use the first and last verses of a long psalm which celebrates God's triumph at the end of the world.

Second Reading   Titus 3:4-7

As at Midnight Mass, this reading is also an excerpt from Paul's letter to Titus. Our salvation is not a reward but a gift from God through Jesus Christ. Even the meaning of God's saving actions needs to be revealed to us.

Gospel   Luke 2:15-20

Luke continues the account of the birth of Jesus by recounting the visit of the shepherds.

The Nativity of the Lord • Years A,B,C
(Mass during the day)

Collect

As the Son of God now shares our humanity, may we share his divinity (which we do through the indwelling of the Trinity and our adoption by God).

First Reading
Isaiah 52:7-10

This passage from Isaiah rejoices in the return of the Jewish exiles to Jerusalem where God will be king, indeed ruler over the world and not only the city. It is applied here to the event celebrated in today's feast.

Psalm 97 (98)

All the ends of the earth have seen the salvation of our God.

Like the psalm at the Dawn Mass, this psalm is an eschatological hymn of praise to God.

Second Reading
Hebrews 1:1-6

The opening verses of the letter to the Hebrews, a letter by an unknown author, probably about 67 AD, and addressed to a group of Jewish Christians. The verses speak of the greatness of Christ, God-made-man, the brightness and the perfect copy of the Father. Hence, identity of nature, distinction of persons.

Gospel
John 1:1-18

This passage is the Prologue of St John's gospel. The Old Testament speaks of God's word, his wisdom, present before the world was made. By it, all things were made. It was sent to the earth to reveal God's hidden plans and to return to God when its mission was fulfilled. It is this divine Word that St John identifies as a divine Person, the incarnate Jesus Christ.

The Holy Family • Year A

The Holy Family is different from every other human family. Is it realistic to present it as the model for our families?

Collect

We ask God to help us to imitate the Holy Family and to practise their virtues in the lives of our own families.

First Reading   Ecclesiasticus 3:2-6.12-14

The book of Ecclesiasticus was written in the second century BC to urge Jews to remain faithful to their own traditions at a time when the fashion in Palestine was hellenisation (that is, adopting Greek manners and customs). Today's passage urges children to honour and cherish their parents.

Psalm 127 (128)

*O blessed are those who fear the Lord
and walk in his ways!*

A Psalm to celebrate the domestic happiness given by God to the virtuous.

Second Reading   Colossians 3:12-21

St Paul, writing to the Christians of Colossae in Asia Minor, reminds them of the rules of good Christian behaviour. The passage ends with some brief specific advice for wives, husbands and their children.

Gospel   Matthew 2:13-15.19-23

From the 'infancy Gospel' in Matthew, we learn some details of the Holy Family's flight from King Herod to Egypt and their return after Herod's death (which occurred in 4 BC). A few final words tell us of their arrival in Nazareth.

Solemnity of Mary, the Holy Mother of God • Years A,B,C

This feast (the Solemnity of Mary, Mother of God) has to 'compete' with (its occurring on) New Year's Day, as well as the eighth day after Christmas (the circumcision of Jesus) and the world day of prayer for peace.

Collect

It was through 'the fruitful virginity' of Mary that God's Son became man. We ask God that, through Mary's intercession, we may gain the salvation won by her Son.

First Reading   Numbers 6:22-27

The book of Numbers is the fourth of the five earliest books of the Old Testament which are called the Pentateuch (and also the Torah). Numbers describes the later part of the Jews' journey through the desert from slavery in Egypt to the Promised Land.

The First Reading today (New Year's Day) uses a solemn blessing of the people, the words of which were given to the Jewish priests by God.

Psalm 66 (67)

O God, be gracious and bless us.

This Psalm was probably used to give thanks for the harvest. It speaks of God's love for all peoples and nations.

Second Reading   Galatians 4:4-7

Galatia is an area in central Anatolia in Asia Minor (now Turkey). St Paul, in the letter to the Galatians, tells us that, through God's Son, born of Mary, we are redeemed and made sons and daughters of God by adoption.

Gospel   Luke 2:16-21

This is the same Gospel passage as at the Dawn Mass of Christmas (the shepherds' visit to the infant Jesus). A final verse is added to record the Saviour's circumcision and formal naming.

Second Sunday after the Nativity • Years A,B,C

The liturgy continues to reflect on the Christmas event, and especially that God's Wisdom is now revealed and its identity made known.

Collect

We pray that God may fill the earth with his glory and make himself known throughout the world.

First Reading   Ecclesiasticus 24:1-2.8-12

Ecclesiasticus (or 'the Book of Sirach', second century BC) was written to combat the spread of pagan Greek influence among Jews.

The passage read is called a eulogy of Wisdom, seen as a reality in union with, but distinct from, the Father. In the New Testament, Wisdom is personified variously as the Second Person (the Word) or the Third Person (the Spirit) or even, as here, as the Blessed Virgin.

Psalm 147

The Word was made flesh,
and lived among us.   or   *Alleluia!*

God has special care of the Jews, his people. He brings freedom, peace and plenty. We pray this Psalm, aware that God's special care is no longer restricted to Jews.

Second Reading   Ephesians 1:3-6.15-18

In his letter to the church in Ephesus (in Asia Minor, near Smyrna/Izmir), St Paul outlines God's eternal plan of salvation for us all. He praises the Ephesians for their faith and love and assures them of his constant prayers.

Gospel   John 1:1-18

This is the Prologue of St John's Gospel (as at the Christmas Mass during the day). In the Old Testament, God's eternal Wisdom/Word is that by which all things come into being; sent to the world to reveal God's loving plans, it will return to him when its mission is fulfilled. St John identifies this Wisdom/Word as Jesus Christ, God become man.

The Epiphany of the Lord • Years A,B,C

A strange and mysterious story, but one with great significance for our understanding of the mission of Jesus Christ.

Collect

On this day when God made his Son known by a star, we pray that the God whom we know now by faith may one day be revealed to us in glory.

First Reading

Isaiah 60:1-6

Isaiah (Deutero-Isaiah or later, see p.13) proclaims the restoration of the glory of Jerusalem. The original context is the return of the Jews from exile. However, the worldwide outlook of the passage is appropriate for the feast celebrating the revelation to gentiles (and not only to Jews) of a divine saviour.

Psalm 71 (72)

All nations shall fall prostrate before you, O Lord.

The Psalm was composed in praise of King Solomon and his reign of justice and peace. Both Jewish and Christian traditions apply the Psalm also to the promised messiah-king.

Second Reading

Ephesians 3:2-3a.5-6

In the letter to the Ephesians, St Paul declares that he has been entrusted with preaching God's plan of salvation. This plan is for all nations, gentiles as well as Jews.

Gospel

Matthew 2:1-12

It is in Matthew's Gospel that we read the account of the visit of the Magi. They were people of wisdom, from somewhere east of Palestine and therefore (an important and significant detail) they were gentiles. There is a long tradition that the gifts bear a certain symbolism for the messiah-king: gold for a royal person, frankincense for a divine person, myrrh for a death and burial.

The Baptism of the Lord • Year A

All four evangelists report this event, implying the importance of recording it as the start of Jesus' public ministry. What is the meaning of Jesus asking to be baptised by John?

Collect

At the baptism of Jesus, the Father declared him his beloved Son. We recall that, by baptism and the Holy Spirit, God has adopted us as his sons and daughters.

First Reading   Isaiah 42:1-4.6-7

From the prophecy of Deutero-Isaiah. Part of 'the first song of the servant of the Lord' which proclaims an unnamed person, chosen to be God's witness before the nations. The New Testament and the Church identify this servant as Jesus.

Psalm 28 (29)

The Lord will bless his people with peace.

We are called to praise God for his glory and power.

Second Reading   Acts 10:34-38

An important incident from the Acts of the Apostles. Peter makes it clear to a family of gentiles that all people are acceptable to God and can be baptised. Jesus did not come as saviour only of the Jewish people.

Gospel   Matthew 3:13-17

St Matthew's account of the baptism of Jesus by John the Baptist. It is an event that shows Christ's humility and his solidarity with us, and also an occasion for a divine revelation of his mission. The feast allows us to reflect on our own baptism and on its effects and purpose.

Lent and Easter, Year A

Ash Wednesday • Years A,B,C

During the seasons of Lent and Easter, the regulations laid down for the selection of readings in Ordinary Time are in abeyance. The readings are chosen for their suitability for a particular day, not for their position in a sequence.

Collect

We pray that, by this day of fasting, our weeks of Lenten conversion and renewal may have an auspicious start.

First Reading   Joel 2:12-18

From the prophecy of Joel (c.400 BC) and originally about a plague of locusts which had laid Judah waste. Today's reading is a call to repentance from God who is ready to forgive and restore.

Psalm 50 (51)

Have mercy on us, O Lord, for we have sinned.

In this penitential psalm, known as the *Miserere*, we confess our sinfulness and confidently ask God to forgive us and restore us to his favour.

Second Reading   2 Corinthians 5:20-6:2

St Paul in his second letter to the Christians of Corinth appeals to them to seek reconciliation with God since God is ready to forgive through the merits of his Son.

Gospel   Matthew 6:1-6.16-18

From that part of St Matthew's Gospel called the Sermon on the Mount. Jesus speaks of the three kinds of good works: almsgiving, prayer and fasting, reminding us that we should not do them in order to win people's admiration. The three activities are means to help us be open to receive the Lenten graces of genuine repentance and a deeper faith.

First Sunday of Lent • Year A

Collect

We pray that, by our Lenten activities, we may discover and gain the riches God has prepared for us.

First Reading   Genesis 2:7-9; 3:1-7

The early chapters of the book of Genesis have two accounts of the creation. This reading is the second, 'Yahwistic', narrative of creation and then of the fall into sin (disobedience) and the consequent loss of innocence. From the start, the human race has been in need of redemption.

Psalm 50 (51)

Have mercy on us, O Lord, for we have sinned.

Repeating the penitential psalm of Ash Wednesday and the same verses from it, we confess our sinfulness and with trust seek God's forgiveness and restored favour.

Second Reading   Romans 5:12-19

In the letter to the Romans, Paul sets out the doctrine of original sin. Through Adam's sin and its consequence, death, we are all born in sin and have to accept death. But Christ, the 'Second Adam' and in parallel with the first Adam, compensates for the disaster. God remakes his creation through his incarnate Son, the new head of the human race and our Saviour.

Gospel   Matthew 4:1-11

St Matthew's account of Jesus' temptations in the wilderness. He was taken there by the Holy Spirit. His rejection of the devil's temptation shows his determination to be a humble messiah, dependent on and obedient to God; not a political messiah with worldly power and wealth.

Second Sunday of Lent • Year A

Collect

We pray to the Father that, having listened to his beloved Son, we may be enabled to witness the Father's glory.

First Reading Genesis 12:1-4a

As God urges us not to settle where we are but to follow his transfigured Son with trust, we read, in the book of Genesis, how God told Abraham to leave home and family and go where God took him. Abraham, trusting God's assurances, obeyed.

Psalm 32 (33)

May your love be upon us, O Lord,
as we place all our hope in you.

We use verses 4 and 5, which speak of a God who is faithful and in whom we can place our complete trust.

Second Reading 2 Timothy 1:8-10

In this second letter to Timothy (whom he had left in charge of the Christians in Ephesus), St Paul speaks of God's eternal plan to save and sanctify us through Christ. This is the Good News which we can trust despite any hardships that come our way.

Gospel Matthew 17:1-9

St Matthew's account of Christ's transfiguration in which the three apostles are privileged to witness Christ's glory as God's Son and the Messiah. Moses and Elijah represent the Law and the Prophets of the Old Testament, doing homage to the founder of the New Testament.

The transfiguration is an event in which God reassures his Son and his closest disciples that all is well despite the journey they are on, leaving the comfort of Galilee for Jerusalem and facing the prospect of suffering and death for Jesus.

Third Sunday of Lent • Year A

We should keep in mind that Lent is not only a season for conversion and for getting ready for Easter, but also a time of preparation for baptism, either to be received or to be remembered with its commitment renewed.

Collect

As sinners, we ask God's mercy, acknowledging also his teaching that fasting, prayer and almsgiving are remedies for sin.

(The Readings for Year A on 3rd, 4th and 5th Sundays of Lent are appropriate for those preparing for baptism at the Easter Vigil. They should be used in parishes and communities in any year when there are to be such baptisms; they can in fact be used each year in any parish or community, if so desired.)

First Reading   Exodus 17:3-7

The reading is from the book of Exodus. The Israelites have escaped from slavery in Egypt and God is guiding them to Palestine, the Promised Land. But in the barren Sinai peninsula they can find no water. At God's instruction, Moses strikes a rock and water gushes out. The life-giving water is, for us, a symbol of baptism.

Psalm 94 (95)

O that today you would listen to his voice:
'Harden not your hearts.'

This psalm starts each day's Divine Office. Here we praise God's loving care of us, with an obvious allusion to the first reading.

Second Reading   Romans 5:1-2.5-8

St Paul, writing to the Roman Christians (chapter 5), teaches that we are justified (made righteous) by faith in Jesus our Saviour. So our hope of salvation is true since God's love has been given to us through the gift of the Holy Spirit.

Gospel   John 4:5-42

St John, in his Gospel, chapter 4, recounts the story of Jesus and the Samaritan woman. The incident is full of strange and appealing details, especially a bizarre conversation between Jesus and the woman; at the end, many of the townspeople believe in him. Again, of course, the passage is relevant to the waters of baptism.

Fourth Sunday of Lent • Year A

Another clear reference to baptism – a blind man is cured by being sent by Jesus to wash in flowing water.

Collect

We ask God to help us to prepare eagerly for the celebration of the Easter mysteries.

First Reading   1 Samuel 16:1.6-7.10-13

David, the youngest son of Jesse of Bethlehem and a shepherd, is chosen by God and anointed by Samuel to be king of Israel.

Psalm 22 (23)

The Lord is my shepherd;
there is nothing I shall want.

This familiar psalm concerning the good shepherd is, of course, in the Old Testament and refers primarily to God. Its allusion to David and, for Christians, to Jesus is evident.

Second Reading   Ephesians 5:8-14

In his letter to the Ephesians, St Paul declares that the light which is Christ will dispel the darkness caused by the lack of faith and by sin.

Gospel   John 9:1-41

Another long narrative from St John (chapter 9), this time about a man born blind to whom Jesus gives sight, both to his eyes and also of faith. Jesus sends the man to wash in the Pool of Siloam (a well in Jerusalem). The man is harassed by various people (neighbours, acquaintances, religious leaders). When Jesus hears of this, he goes in search of the man to comfort him – a reaction that typifies Christ. The connection with baptism (washing with water, the gift of faith/sight) is clear.

Fifth Sunday of Lent • Year A

*'Living water' was offered by Jesus to the woman at the well; 'go and wash
at the pool' was Jesus' instruction to the blind man; and (today) a man who
was dead hears Jesus say 'unbind him, let him go free'. Memorable teaching
on the meaning and effect of baptism.*

Collect

We ask God to give us the kind of love that enabled his Son to sacrifice his
life for our sake.

First Reading   Ezekiel 37:12-14

The prophet Ezekiel (sixth century BC) has a vision of God bringing dead
bones to life again. The primary reference is to the Jews returning to their own
land after exile in Babylon. It also is understood as the resurrection of Israel at
the coming of the messiah and an early sign of a belief in individual resurrection of the body after death. This reading, evidently, relates to today's Gospel
(and to Christ's work of salvation).

Psalm 129 (130)

> *With the Lord there is mercy
> and fullness of redemption.*

The *De Profundis* (Out of the Depths) is a psalm of hope. It is used in our
prayers for those who have died and expresses our trust in God's merciful love.

Second Reading   Romans 8:8-11

In the letter to the Romans (ch. 8), St Paul speaks of the Holy Spirit dwelling in
us. Just as Jesus was restored to human life through the Spirit, so the same Spirit
living in us will give us life (even though we may have been dead through sin).

Gospel   John 11:1-45

Again, a long gospel narrative from St John (chapter 11). Jesus raises Lazarus,
his friend who has died, to life. The purpose of the miracle is to strengthen our
faith; not only that those who die will, in a distant future, live again, but that life
continues for us after our bodies are dead. Those, whose bodies we bury and
leave after their death, are alive and with God. The miracle of the resurrection
of Lazarus is the sign of Christ's dominance over death. (The choice of this passage just before Holy Week is no coincidence, of course.)

Palm Sunday of the Passion of the Lord • Years A,B,C

Blessing of Palms

Before Mass, there is a Liturgy of the Word entitled **The Commemoration of the Lord's Entry into Jerusalem.**

One of two **Prayers** is chosen for the blessing of the branches:

(a) As we accompany Christ our King today, we pray that he may lead us on to the eternal Jerusalem.

(b) As with these branches we greet Christ today, we pray that, through him, we may produce the fruit of good works.

Gospel of the Lord's Entrance

Year A: Matthew 21:1-11 • Year B: Mark 11:1-10* • Year C: Luke 19:28-40

In each case and in generally similar terms, the gospels relate how the colt was obtained on which Jesus rode, followed by a description of his entry in triumph from the Mount of Olives into Jerusalem.

*In **Year B, John 12:12-16** is offered as an alternative. It is shorter than the synoptics' accounts, describing only Christ's entry into Jerusalem.

At Mass: Collect

We pray that, by following the example of Christ's humble and patient suffering, we may also share in the glory of his resurrection.

First Reading   Isaiah 50:4-7

In the prophecy of Deutero-Isaiah are the four 'songs of the servant of the Lord', depicting a perfect disciple who proclaims the true faith and undergoes suffering to atone for the people's sins, and whom God finally raises in triumph. Constant Christian tradition sees these as prophecies foretelling the life, death and resurrection of Jesus. This reading is the third of the 'songs'.

Psalm 21 (22)

My God, my God, why have you forsaken me?

This psalm is the lament of an innocent but persecuted person who begs God's help and is finally rescued from his suffering. The first line of the psalm is today's response and also is one of Christ's 'seven last words on the cross' (Matthew 27:46). For this, it is seen as messianic and anticipating episodes in Our Lord's passion.

Second Reading   Philippians 2:6-11

From St Paul's letter to the church at Philippi (in the north of Greece). This extract is a hymn, probably of unknown authorship but quoted by St Paul, which praises Jesus Christ, truly God, by noting the various stages of his human life – incarnation, passion and death, resurrection, universal recognition as 'Lord' (a word which is a divine title).

Gospel
Year A: Matthew 26:14-27:66 • Year B: Mark 14:1-15:47
Year C: Luke 22:14-23:56

Each evangelist's account of the Last Supper, the agony in Gethsemane, Our Lord's arrest and trial, passion, death and burial.

[The Passover supper was due to be eaten on the Friday of Holy Week (see John 18:28 and other texts) but Matthew, Mark and Luke (the synoptic Gospels) speak of the Thursday Last Supper as the Passover supper. That meal had a paschal liturgy (see Mark 14:22-26). Perhaps Jesus, knowing that he would be unable to eat it the following day, decided to anticipate it on the Thursday.]

Thursday of the Lord's Supper • Years A,B,C

Jesus washed the apostles' feet at the Last Supper. He asked them to copy him in similar loving service for others. Do you not think that, at this evening's Eucharist, loving service will be shown not only by the person who washes others' feet, but also by those who agree to have their feet washed?

Collect

As we celebrate the eucharistic sacrifice instituted by Jesus on the eve of his passion and death, we pray that, by this great mystery, we may gain the fullness of love and life.

First Reading   Exodus 12:1-8.11-14

In the book of Exodus, God describes how the Israelites have to eat the Passover supper. Each year it will commemorate their escape from slavery in Egypt. The Jewish Passover, for Christians, is fulfilled in the Eucharist: Christ is the Lamb of God, sacrificed on Calvary and eaten at the Last Supper and thus bringing salvation to the world (and coinciding with the annual Jewish Passover festival).

[The word Passover, for Jews, refers primarily to God 'passing over' (omitting, bypassing) their houses on his mission of death; and also their 'passing' from slavery to freedom. For Christians it came to mean Christ's work of salvation and explicitly his 'passing' from death to resurrection and his return to the Father (and also our passing from this life to eternal life). The word 'pasch' is derived, through the Greek, from the Hebrew for 'Passover'; hence the phrase, 'Paschal Mystery'.]

Psalm 115 (116)

The blessing-cup that we bless
is a communion with the blood of Christ

A psalm of thanksgiving with phrases seen by Christians as prophetic allusions to Christ's work of salvation.

Second Reading   1 Corinthians 11:23-26

In his first (still extant) letter to the Christians in Corinth, St Paul briefly describes the heart of the Eucharist: bread and wine provide the signs of the new and eternal covenant between God and his people.

[This is the earliest written account of the Eucharist, preceding the Gospel narratives.]

Gospel   John 13:1-15

St John's account of the Last Supper omits the institution of the Eucharist (told in the synoptics and 1st Corinthians). Only John tells us that Jesus washed the apostles' feet. This action is an expression of Christ's humble love for his disciples (an action to be copied at the eucharistic celebration this evening). Jesus asks us to show the same love in the service of our brothers and sisters.

The Celebration of the Passion of the Lord • Years A,B,C

Opening Prayer

We pray to the Father that we, for whom his Son suffered and died, may be made holy and that, as Christ became human like us, we in turn may be made images of him.

First Reading   Isaiah 52:13-53:12

This is the last of the 'four songs of the servant of the Lord' and is found in the prophecy of Deutero-Isaiah (chapter 52, final three verses, and all of chapter 53). The songs tell us of a person who is specially destined to be God's servant, a teacher, a leader and a judge of humankind but who will humbly endure great suffering. In this fourth song, the servant will suffer though innocent, and will be condemned to death which he will offer on behalf of sinners. The Lord accepts this offering for the human race and the servant will be recognised as triumphant. Christian tradition, of course, identifies the suffering servant as Jesus our Saviour.

Psalm 30 (31)

Father, into your hands I commend my spirit.

This psalm is of a person who is enduring an ordeal. The response is verse 5 of the psalm and Luke's Gospel tells us that they were the final words of Jesus as he died. Several other verses of the psalm are used in today's responsorial psalm.

Second Reading   Hebrews 4:14-16; 5:7-9

From the letter to the Hebrews, author unknown, written probably around 67 AD, for some Jewish Christians. Today's reading is from parts of chapters 4 and 5. Jesus is our high priest and, because human as well as divine, he experienced weakness and suffering. His prayers and entreaties are therefore effective with God and obtain for us eternal salvation.

Gospel   John 18:1-19:42

St John's account of Gethsemane and Our Lord's arrest, trials, crucifixion, death and burial. In John's Gospel, Christ is presented as divine but with details of his true humanity as well. It records the Christ of history but as one who is, and knows he is, the saviour of the world; even the crucifixion is part of Christ's exaltation. The Gospel contains a lot of symbolism but the symbols are also real historical events; the symbolism explains the inner meaning of the events. (All four evangelists relate that, before being taken to Pilate for trial and condemnation, Jesus was arraigned for questioning before Jewish religious authorities. However, in their accounts of these preliminary hearings, the four evangelists give differing details regarding the place, day and identity of the authorities concerned.)

The Easter Vigil • Years A, B, C

The seven Old Testament readings for use at the Easter Vigil comprise three readings describing crucial stages in God's care of his people in preparation for the coming of his Son as our saviour and four passages which the Homiletic Directory of the Holy See (no.48) describes as 'pivotal themes of the prophets' for a deeper understanding of the Paschal Mystery.

First Reading   From the Book of Genesis (1:1-2:2): God's work of creating the universe, including man.

Second Reading   From the Book of Genesis (22:1-18): In obedience to God, Abraham is prepared to offer his own son in sacrifice, but at the last moment God gives him a ram to sacrifice in place of Isaac.

Third Reading   From the Book of Exodus (14:15-15:1): The Jews, led by Moses, end their exile and slavery in Egypt when God divides the Red Sea to allow them to pass through while the pursuing Egyptian army is caught and drowned.

Fourth Reading   From the Prophet Isaiah (54:5-14): God declares that he loves his people, the Jews, so much that he sees himself as a husband reconciled with his erring but repentant wife.

Fifth Reading   From the Prophet Isaiah (55:1-11): God loves his covenanted people and all humankind. He will show his love by his care for them, providing them with their needs.

Sixth Reading   From the Prophet Baruch (3:9-15.32-4:4): God laments that Israel is exiled from him. He calls them back to his presence and love.

Seventh Reading   From the Prophet Ezekiel (36:16-28): God sends a saviour to bring Israel back from exile and defilement. He will restore them to the land he gave them and they will be his covenanted people.

Collect

As we celebrate the resurrection of the Lord, we ask God to foster in us, his Church and his adopted children, a desire to serve him faithfully.

New Testament Reading   Romans 6:3-11

St Paul, writing to the Romans, explains that at baptism we die to sin. In a sense (especially vivid if baptism is by immersion into a font), when we are baptised we go into the tomb with the dead Christ so, as he was raised from the dead, we too are raised to live a new life. And, since sinning ends with death, we also must consider ourselves free from the slavery of sin.

Psalm 117 (118)

Alleluia, alleluia, alleluia!

The psalm was sung as a processional hymn of thanksgiving for the Jewish feast of tabernacles. Clearly it is appropriate for the feast of the resurrection.

Gospel

[The four Gospels show divergences in recounting appearances of the risen Christ. There is agreement about the initial appearance of a messenger but that is all. Some reported appearances are to individuals (and these indicate the fact of the resurrection) while others are to groups (and these are to direct work and missions to be undertaken). Nor is there unanimity about the places of the appearances, Mark and Matthew and John chapter 21 indicating Galilee, Luke and John chapter 20 on the other hand indicating Judea. It is claimed that these divergences of traditions are better witnesses of historicity than a contrived uniformity would have been.]

Year A   Matthew 28:1-10

St Matthew narrates that, early on the Sunday morning, two women went to the tomb in which Jesus had been buried and there met an angel who told them that Jesus had risen. They hurry to tell the disciples and, on the way, they meet the risen Lord.

Year B   Mark 16:1-7

The Easter Vigil gospel this year is Mark's account of the women going early on the Sunday morning to anoint the Lord's body in the tomb. On their arrival, the tomb is open, the body not there but a young man/angel tells them that Jesus has risen. They are to tell the disciples and they will see him in Galilee. Contrary to the other three gospels which say that the women did tell the disciples, Mark reports that they were so afraid that they told no one (16:8). The explanation of this is unknown to us, but there are various additional endings to Mark's gospel, one of which (Mark 16:9-20) is held by the Catholic Church as authentic, though probably by an unknown author.

Year C   Luke 24:1-12

From the gospel according to Luke. The women from Galilee, faithful followers of Jesus, went to the tomb to complete the burial of the body of Jesus. Astonished, they saw that the body had been removed. Two men (Matthew says 'an angel', Mark 'a man') suddenly appeared and told them that the Lord had risen. The men reminded them that Jesus had foretold his death and also his resurrection. The women told the Eleven what they had seen and heard, but the apostles and other disciples would not believe them. Luke tells us that Peter (John says 'Peter and John') went to the tomb and saw that it was indeed empty.

Easter Sunday • Years A, B, C

Collect

As we celebrate Christ's resurrection by which he conquered death and opened the way to eternal life for us, we pray that we may, through the Holy Spirit, obtain that life which Our Lord has won for us.

First Reading   Acts 10:34.37-43

From the Acts of the Apostles. The scene is at the house in Caesarea Maritima of Cornelius, a Roman centurion. Cornelius, his family and friends are present as Peter speaks to them. He is telling them about Jesus, adding that Jesus has ordered his disciples to be his witnesses. At first the apostles had restricted their preaching to Jews but this experience of meeting with gentiles has convinced Peter that salvation is for the gentiles also.

Psalm 117 (118)

> *This day was made by the Lord;*
> *we rejoice and are glad.*   or   *Alleluia, alleluia, alleluia!*

The psalm is the same as that sung at the Easter Vigil.

Second Reading   Colossians 3:1-4 or 1 Corinthians 5:6-8

> *There is a choice of readings.*

Colossians 3:1-4: Since we are baptised, we share the risen life of Jesus Christ. We should behave accordingly.

1 Corinthians 5:6-8: Jews removed all yeast from their homes when celebrating Passover. For Christians, Christ is the constant Passover and so we should remove from our lives the 'yeast' of sin.

Gospel   John 20:1-9

Mary Magdalene finds the tomb empty and hurries to tell Peter and John. They verify this and then faith dawns: Jesus is alive – he had to rise from the dead!

At the heart of the Church, we have an unjustly crucified victim of whom God has approved and to whom he has done justice.

Second Sunday of Easter • Year A

> *It is noteworthy that the Roman Missal (2011) gives an alternative designation for this Sunday: 'The Sunday of Divine Mercy'.*

Collect

We seek a deeper faith and a better appreciation of God's generous gifts to us, namely, Christ our redeemer, the Holy Spirit who gives us new life, and baptism itself by which we have access to Jesus and the Spirit.

First Reading   Acts 2:42-47

From the Acts of the Apostles (as all first readings are until Pentecost). A description of the practice of the first Christian community in Jerusalem. In addition to Liturgies of the Word and of the Eucharist, the close nature of the community is notable.

Psalm 117 (118)

> *Give thanks to the Lord for he is good,*
> *for his love has no end.* or *Alleluia, alleluia, alleluia!*

This psalm is a hymn of thanksgiving sung as Jews entered the temple in procession.

Second Reading   1 Peter 1:3-9

All seven Sundays of Easter (in Year A) have extracts from the first letter of Peter for their second readings. The letter (originally perhaps a sermon or homily) is addressed to early gentile convert Christians at a time of persecution or suffering for them. It speaks of baptism as being the source of our new life and of the way in which we should behave, both individually and in community, as Christians.

The author identifies himself as the apostle Peter, but scholars are divided about this. In today's passage, we are urged to respond properly to the gifts received from God.

Gospel   John 20:19-31

In John's Gospel, we read of two appearances of Jesus to the apostles in Jerusalem, the first on the first Easter Sunday and the second (when Thomas, absent earlier, was present) on the following Sunday. On the first occasion, Jesus confers the Holy Spirit on the apostles with the power of forgiving sin; on the second, Thomas humbly confesses his faith in the risen Lord. Jesus declares that the Gospel itself, which is the power of God, will be and is the adequate motive of our faith.

Note that, just as the apostles were slow to believe, merely on others' testimony, that the Lord had risen, Jesus can be hidden even in the Church today; it is our task to place him clearly at the heart of our communities.

Third Sunday of Easter • Year A

Collect

As we rejoice in our adoption as God's children, we look forward to even greater rejoicing at the resurrection of our bodies.

First Reading   Acts 2:14.22-33

From the Acts of the Apostles. It is Pentecost day and Peter is preaching to the crowd. He tells them about Jesus who, though killed, was raised to life by God.

Psalm 15 (16)

Show us, Lord, the path of life. or *Alleluia!*

The psalm declares that the Lord is our heritage and our protector. Our total commitment to God seeks an everlasting union. The psalm indicates a belief in a resurrection, though still vaguely. The psalm was seen as messianic even in pre-Christian Judaism.

Second Reading   1 Peter 1:17-21

Taken from the first letter of Peter. The ransom paid to gain our freedom from sinfulness was a precious one: the blood of Christ. God raised him from the dead and glorified him; this was so that we might have faith and hope in God. These gifts are to be treasured because the ransom was so valuable.

Gospel   Luke 24:13-35

A favourite resurrection appearance: the Emmaus story (from Luke). A story of faith lost and then regained, through being reminded of the Old Testament teaching especially about Christ's words and actions, followed by the nourishment of the Eucharist. This is a story for all of us whose faith is weak. Note the sequel: they hurry to share their recovered faith with others.

Fourth Sunday of Easter • Year A

Although today we pray especially for those whom God calls to the ordained priesthood and to consecrated life, do not be misled: God calls all of us who are baptised to be active and effective witnesses of his Son.

Collect

Our Good Shepherd has gone to eternal life. We ask God that the sheep of the flock may follow him there.

First Reading   Acts 2:14.36-41

In the Acts of the Apostles, the account of the preaching of Peter, about which we heard last Sunday, is continued. The crowd is moved and Peter tells them that they must repent of their sins and be baptised. Three thousand receive the gift of faith and are baptised.

Psalm 22 (23)

> *The Lord is my Shepherd;*
> *there is nothing I shall want.*   or   *Alleluia!*

This well-known psalm uses two images: the shepherd and the host inviting us to a messianic banquet. Christians apply these images to baptism and Eucharist.

Second Reading   1 Peter 2:20-25

Again from the first letter of Peter, we are reminded that Jesus suffered greatly but without complaint, though he was innocent. He acted thus so that our sins might be forgiven and removed. We had strayed from our shepherd but have now returned. We should imitate Jesus in accepting suffering even after doing our duty.

Gospel   John 10:1-10

The Good Shepherd image is in John's Gospel, chapter 10. However, before using the image of the shepherd himself (in Years B and C), Jesus employs a related image in today's excerpt. He is the gate through which shepherds should lead their sheep. (Jesus is speaking to some pharisees but they did not understand his message.) Since in the Old Testament God the Father is often called, or calls himself, a shepherd, Jesus can speak of himself as the gate of the sheepfold (as, in our prayers, we pray to the Father 'through Christ our Lord'). Moreover, 'gate' does not mean a barrier but rather an entrance, an opening into the sheepfold. There are three consequences to Jesus being the gate or door for the sheep:

1. This is the right way to enter if we want to be saved;
2. We can come and go through the door, for we are free, guided by the Spirit;
3. Through the door we shall find pasture, good and abundant nourishment.

Fifth Sunday of Easter • Year A

Collect

We ask God to bring the paschal mystery to fulfilment in us so that, after baptism, we may advance in goodness and reach eternal happiness.

First Reading   Acts 6:1-7

On previous Sundays we have heard, from chapter two of the Acts of the Apostles, about the growth of the early Church in Jerusalem. Today we continue on the same general theme but specifically about the choice of the first deacons and their ordination to take charge of the community's works of charity.

Psalm 32 (33)

May your love be upon us, O Lord,
as we place all our hope in you.   or   *Alleluia!*

A psalm of praise and thanksgiving to God.

Second Reading   1 Peter 2:4-9

Continuing with passages from the first letter of Peter, we read that Christ is the living cornerstone of the living stones that are built into a spiritual edifice for God. We must keep close to Jesus for we are chosen, set apart, consecrated to form a holy and royal priesthood.

Gospel   John 14:1-12

Today's gospel is from John, chapter 14. The setting is the Last Supper and the Lord's farewell discourse to the apostles. His words console them and calm their anxiety at what is happening. He speaks about his going to his Father and that we will follow. The apostles are puzzled and Jesus reassures them that he himself is the way, the truth and the life. Indeed, the life and actions of Jesus make his Father present and visible.

Sixth Sunday of Easter • Year A

Collect

May our celebration and remembrance of Christ's saving death and resurrection bring us joy and always guide our lives in accordance with what is right.

First Reading   Acts 8:5-8.14-17

The passage is from chapter 8 of the Acts of the Apostles. The deacon Philip goes north to a Samaritan town and preaches. Many are converted and Peter and John arrive to confer the gift of the Spirit. This story illustrates the early spread of Christianity, specifically to people who, though regarded by Jews as heretics, also awaited a messiah.

[There is a problem about baptism 'in the name of the Lord Jesus' which did not give the Holy Spirit. Perhaps it is a rather clumsy attempt to insist on the need to involve the Twelve to whom the Spirit was given at Pentecost.]

Psalm 65 (66)

Cry out with joy to God all the earth.   or   *Alleluia!*

The verses we use are selected from a psalm which gives thanksgiving to God on behalf of the entire community.

Second Reading   1 Peter 3:15-18

The passage, from the first letter of Peter, speaks of the unashamed hope we have because of Jesus Christ. And if we suffer from others, so did Christ – and for our sins.

Gospel   John 14:15-21

We continue from last Sunday to hear Our Lord's discourse at the Last Supper. He promises us the Holy Spirit to be our protector, since he himself will no longer be physically and visibly with us. But because the three Persons have a shared life, Jesus (and the Father) will be with the Spirit; moreover, because we have faith in Jesus and love him, he is mysteriously but truly present with us. We share his life as he shares the Father's life.

The Ascension of the Lord • Years A,B,C

Collect

We rejoice in this celebration, aware that the ascension of Christ is a pledge of our own eternal destiny with him.

First Reading   Acts 1:1-11

At the very start of the Acts of the Apostles, St Luke describes the days after the resurrection when Jesus instructed the apostles. Note that they were asked to bear public witness to Jesus, his teaching, his death and resurrection. The importance of proclaiming correctly the kingdom which Jesus has inaugurated is clear. The passage ends with a brief description of the ascension itself.

Psalm 46 (47)

God goes up with shouts of joy;
the Lord goes up with trumpet blast.   or   *Alleluia!*

The psalm is a hymn of acclamation for the Lord, the King of Israel, as he goes in triumph to his temple. The people in fact acclaim him as ruler of all nations, one day to be recognised as such by everyone.

Second Reading   Ephesians 1:17-23

In the Letter to the Ephesians St Paul assures us of what God has prepared for us to inherit. We know this because of God's power evident in his raising of Christ from the dead and giving him a supreme triumph in eternal life.

Gospel Year A   Matthew 28:16-20

The final verses of St Matthew's Gospel do not expressly speak of the ascension. Rather, Jesus reassures the apostles and reminds them of all they have learned as his disciples. They will be responsible for passing on their experience of him. They will tell of the risen Christ, proclaim the Good News, and establish communities. But their basic mission will be to make disciples of Jesus, baptising people who will live with the same ideals as his and be strengthened by his presence.

• Alternative Second Reading for Year B   Ephesians 4:1-13

In this excerpt from the letter to the Ephesians, Paul is appealing to Christians to maintain their unity in Christ. Each of us is given the gift of graces allotted to us by Christ to carry out different tasks in the Church so that, working together, we build the one body of Christ. Speaking of Christ going to heaven for this purpose, Paul quotes psalm 67 (68), verse 18.

Gospel for Year B   Mark 16:15-20

The final verses of Mark's gospel (16:9-20) are problematic. Although probably of different authorship, the Church however accepts them as authentic. Today's passage (16:15-20) speaks of the mission to proclaim the Good News worldwide. The accompanying signs indicate that God's kingdom is already established. The Eleven did 'preach everywhere' and Jesus, to whom the divine word 'Lord' is attached, was helping them.

• Alternative Second Reading for Year C   Hebrews 9:24-28; 10:19-23

The Jewish high priest, and he alone, entered the holy of holies each year to offer animal blood as a sacrifice for sin. Christ, however, entered into God's presence with his own blood as sacrifice for our sins. That sacrifice needed to be made only once. When he comes again it will not be for another self-sacrifice but as our judge. Moreover, entry to God's presence is now available to us all, through Christ's blood shed for us.

Gospel for Year C   Luke 24:46-53

In Luke's gospel, Jesus, after reminding the disciples of the mission that he was bequeathing them, took them just outside of Jerusalem, blessed them and was taken up to heaven. They returned, full of joy, to the city and went often to the temple to praise God.

[On the Mount of Olives, there is a white, flat stone in the ground with two footmarks impressed on it. They are shown as the footprints of Jesus as he took off, heaven bound.]

Seventh Sunday of Easter • Year A

Collect

We believe that Jesus our Saviour is with the Father in glory and we pray that he may also and always be present with us here on earth.

First Reading   Acts 1:12-14

From the Acts of the Apostles, telling us that, after Jesus' ascension, the apostles returned to Jerusalem and there, with Mary, the mother of Jesus, and some others, they 'joined in continuous prayer'.

[Note that Matthew located Jesus' final words to the apostles in Galilee, while Luke says that Jesus ascended from the Mount of Olives, near Jerusalem. The writers were interested not so much in geographical accuracy as in adorning their accounts with elements of symbolism.]

Psalm 26 (27)

I am sure I shall see the Lord's goodness
in the land of the living.   or   *Alleluia!*

The psalm verses that we use in this Mass express our desire to be with God and declare that, in his presence, there is no fear.

Second Reading   1 Peter 4:13-16

In a further reading from the first letter of Peter, we are taught that suffering with and for Christ is a blessing and will bring its reward. To be punished for evil deeds would be shameful but deserved; to suffer for being a Christian is an honour.

Gospel   John 17:1-11

From chapter 17 of St John's Gospel, today's extract is the first part of Christ's priestly prayer to his Father at the Last Supper. Jesus speaks of having completed the work the Father gave him. He prays for the apostles; they have accepted his teaching and believe that he was sent by the Father. Jesus tells his Father that he is coming to him and prays that, as he has glorified the Father while on earth, the Father will now glorify him.

Pentecost Sunday • Years A,B,C

Collect

The Holy Spirit came and comes still to sanctify the Church in every nation. We pray that there may be a renewed outpouring of the Spirit's gifts across the whole earth and in the hearts of all believers.

First Reading   Acts 2:1-11

We hear Luke's account in Acts of the coming of the Spirit on the apostles and on those with them (cf. first reading, last Sunday) and the wonderful conversions which resulted from their preaching.

[Note that those converted were all Jews or proselytes, the latter being gentiles who were circumcised in order to convert to Judaism.]

Psalm 103 (104)

Send forth your Spirit, O Lord,
and renew the face of the earth.   or   *Alleluia!*

This psalm delights in the variety and glory of God's creation, but the verses chosen for today's liturgy concentrate on praising God and his Spirit, God's instrument of creation.

Second Reading   1 Corinthians 12:3-7.12-13

In his first letter to the Christians in Corinth, St Paul speaks of the Holy Spirit. Since in the Church there are many tasks to be done, it is necessary that the Spirit gives us a range of different gifts. Just as a human person is one body in spite of having many parts, so also is the Church, the mystical body of Christ, one; and indeed there is one Spirit from whom come the many gifts.

Gospel   John 20:19-23

We read in St John's Gospel how the risen Jesus gave the apostles the task of continuing the same mission as he had inaugurated. For them to be successful, he gave them the Spirit. He did this by breathing on them; the action of breathing on someone has, in the Scriptures, a special role of empowering. In fact, in Hebrew, the word *ruah* is used for both 'spirit' and 'breath'.

[John sees the connection between the resurrection of Jesus and the empowerment of the Church by the Spirit to be so close and intimate that he disregards any chronological consideration and considers the two events to be on the same day.]

Alternative Second Readings and Gospels for Years B and C overleaf.

• Alternative Second Reading for Year B   Galatians 5:16-25

The Holy Spirit guides us in our lives so that we behave in a manner that is virtuous and exemplary. Without the Spirit, self-indulgence takes control and the result is a life of bad behaviour.

Alternative Gospel for Year B   John 15:26-27; 16:12-15

In his discourse to the apostles at the Last Supper, Jesus promises to send 'the Spirit of truth', 'the Advocate', to be with them as his witness. With the truth that comes from both the Father and Jesus himself, the Spirit will glorify Christ by leading the apostles into 'the complete truth'. Jesus adds that, from the Spirit, they will learn of 'the things to come', an expression referring to the full meaning of Christ's death and resurrection (which, at the Last Supper, were still ahead).

• Alternative Second Reading for Year C   Romans 8:8-17

Paul teaches that, with Christ in us, the Holy Spirit also dwells in us and ensures our immortality. Having the Spirit in us makes us the sons and daughters of God, with the right to acclaim God as our Father and, as his children by adoption, to be coheirs with Christ.

Alternative Gospel for Year C   John 14:15-16.23-26

At the Last Supper, on the eve of his death, Jesus gives his farewell discourse to the apostles. He asks them to show their love for him by keeping his commandments and promises that he and the Father will show their love for them by dwelling in them. More than that, the Holy Spirit, the Advocate, will be sent to them by the Father in Jesus' name, to remain with them as their teacher and to remind them of all that Jesus has told them.

The Most Holy Trinity • Year A

The Trinity is the most mysterious of all mysteries, totally beyond our comprehension. However, God has revealed some aspects of the mystery. We should be anxious to know these aspects as well as venerating and adoring the one God of three Persons, equal in eternity and majesty.

Collect

As God revealed the mystery of the Trinity by sending into our world the divine Word and the Holy Spirit, we pray that we may believe with faith that God is one in nature but three distinct Persons, Father, Son and Spirit.

First Reading   Exodus 34:4-6.8-9

From the book of Exodus. Moses meets God the Lord on Mount Sinai. He
declares himself to be a God of tenderness and compassion. God constantly
warned the Jews against polytheism, so common among the pagans.

Psalm   Daniel 3:52-56

To you glory and praise for evermore.

In the book of Daniel (second century BC), we learn about the three young
men, exiled Jews in the service of King Nebuchadnezzar of Babylon (sixth
century BC). They are unharmed in the midst of a furnace. They sing God's
praises and glorify him.

Second Reading   2 Corinthians 13:11-13

Today's reading is the conclusion of St Paul's second letter to the Corinthians. It is used especially because of the trinitarian formula with which it ends.
Several of St Paul's letters either begin with a similarly worded greeting or end
with a similar farewell, but this is a particularly explicit example.

Gospel   John 3:16-18

In John's Gospel, chapter 3, a long conversation is reported between Jesus and
Nicodemus, 'a leading Jew'. Nicodemus is puzzled by Jesus declaring solemnly
that, to have eternal life, we must be 'born from above'. (This phrase refers to
baptism by which we receive the Holy Spirit.) In this short extract from the
dialogue Jesus tells Nicodemus that God sent his Son to the world so that all
may gain eternal life if they believe in him. This shows the love that God has
for every one of us (and implies the Spirit of love that animates God).

The Most Holy Body and Blood of Christ • Year A

*Although Holy Thursday and the Mass of the Lord's Supper solemnly commemorate
Christ's gift of the Eucharist, our awareness that the following day is Good Friday
overshadows our celebration that day of the Eucharist's institution. So this feast was
inaugurated in the thirteenth century, first in Liége and then throughout the world.
Pope Urban IV commissioned St Thomas Aquinas to compose the texts for the
feast; they include the hymns* Lauda Sion *and* Pange Lingua *(the final two verses
of which are sung at Benediction:* Tantum ergo Sacramentum*).*

Collect

On this feast, the Collect is addressed to God the Son. We pray to him that we may be so devoted to the sacred mystery of the Eucharist as to receive the graces won by him in his work of salvation.

First Reading   Deuteronomy 8:2-3.14-16

In the book of Deuteronomy, Moses reminds the people of their years of journeying in the wilderness and that, while they endured the sufferings of those years, God was their protector who also gave them manna for their food and, in the arid desert, water to drink. Christian tradition sees the Eucharist as the fulfilment of God's providing the Jews with life-giving food and drink.

Psalm 147

O praise the Lord, Jerusalem! or *Alleluia!*

The psalm is in praise of God, especially because he is the liberator and friend of Israel. Note especially a verse particularly appropriate for today's feast: He feeds you with finest wheat.

Second Reading   1 Corinthians 10:16-17

In this short reading from 1st Corinthians, chapter 10, Paul speaks of the bread and wine being a communion with the body and blood of Christ; and the use of a single loaf being a symbol of the unity of the many participants. [I think that, nowadays, neither 'one' nor 'loaf' is helpful in making the intended point.]

Gospel   John 6:51-58

In John, chapter 6, Jesus speaks plainly about holy communion. We eat his flesh and drink his blood; this ensures that we have life drawn from Jesus that will enable us to live for ever. The celebration of Mass allows us to have Jesus present with us, to hear and ponder his teaching and to 'communicate' with him in order to nourish our faith and to become more identified with him. Note also how Christ's words encourage us to receive holy communion under both kinds.

Sundays 2-34 in Ordinary Time, Year A

Second Sunday in Ordinary Time • Year A

Collect

We ask God the all-powerful to give peace to the world.

First Reading   Isaiah 49:3.5-6

This reading is taken from the prophecy of Deutero-Isaiah and is part of the second 'song of the servant of the Lord'. The servant will be the saviour not only of the Jews but of all the nations of the world.

Psalm 39 (40)

Here I am, Lord!
I come to do your will.

We praise God for making his will known to us and thank him that we have been obedient.

Second Reading   1 Corinthians 1:1-3

For the next seven Sundays, the second readings are from 1st Corinthians, chapters 1-4. St Paul introduces himself to the Christians of Corinth, a Greek coastal city where the Christians faced great temptations against their faith and morals.

Gospel   John 1:29-34

As an exception for this Sunday of Year A, the gospel is from St John, not St Matthew. The passage emphasises the difference between the baptism of John the Baptist and that of Jesus. Jesus has the Holy Spirit dwelling within him and his baptism (in contrast to that of John) confers on us that same Holy Spirit – the Spirit that brings gifts, new life and a new relationship to Christ. So our baptism is not only for forgiveness and reconciliation but also to consecrate us as sacred people with a sacred mission.

Third Sunday in Ordinary Time • Year A

Collect

The opening prayer asks the Father to guide us so that all our activities may be done in the name of Jesus and be pleasing to God.

First Reading   Isaiah 8:23-9:3

The Jews of the Northern Kingdom, grieving and suffering, have been deported by the Assyrians to exile (8th century BC). They are given hope by the promise of liberation and recovered prosperity. For Christians, this prophecy is messianic and is fulfilled in Jesus.

Psalm 26 (27)

The Lord is my light and my help.

A psalm of longing and firm hope. To be with God is our fondest desire.

Second Reading   1 Corinthians 1:10-13.17

After his introduction and greeting (which we heard last Sunday), St Paul urges the Corinth Christians to stop quarrelling among themselves and not to have factions.

It is Christ and his teaching that matter, not the different people who bring the Good News.

Gospel   Matthew 4:12-23

For all the remaining 'Ordinary Sundays' of this year (from 3rd to 34th), we shall work our way through St Matthew's account of Christ's public life and ministry (from his first adult appearance in Galilee to just before his passion and death). The sequence will, of course, be interrupted throughout Lent and Eastertide.

Jesus begins with a summary of his entire teaching: 'Repent, for the kingdom of heaven is close at hand.'

[NB 1. Although he was an itinerant preacher, Jesus based himself at Capernaum on the shores of the Sea of Galilee, rather than in his home hillside village of Nazareth. The people of the latter seemed to lack warmth towards him but, more importantly, Capernaum was then a much busier place and with much better communications.

NB 2. Matthew uses the term 'kingdom of heaven' not to indicate that 'the kingdom of God' (as the other evangelists call it) was deferred until after our death. Since Matthew was writing initially for converts from Judaism for whom the divine name had been so sacred that it was not spoken, he courteously substitutes a euphemism.]

Fourth Sunday in Ordinary Time • Year A

Collect

We pray to be able to give God genuine honour and to have a sincere love for everyone.

First Reading   Zephaniah 2:3; 3:12-13

From one of the so-called twelve minor prophets: Zephaniah (7th century BC). The prophet foresees a day when a remnant of Israelites will live humble and virtuous lives under God's protection.

Psalm 145 (146)

How happy are the poor in spirit;
theirs is the kingdom of heaven.

The Lord is faithful and protects the poor and all those in need.

Second Reading   1 Corinthians 1:26-31

God chooses those who, by human standards, are foolish, weak and of little account. Joined to Christ, we are able to be sharers of his wisdom and holiness.

Gospel   Matthew 5:1-12

Today we begin to hear the Sermon on the Mount (Matthew 5, 6 & 7).

The passage today is a list of the 'beatitudes', the eighth and last being expanded by a later explanatory addition. The beatitudes are descriptions of the qualities needed in us to be good members of God's kingdom which Jesus came to establish. The qualities are characteristic of the poor and powerless, the opposite of the conventional values of the world. God's kingdom, therefore, will involve a moral revolution, turning common standards upside down.

The beatitudes illustrate that Jesus came not to abolish the precepts of the Old Law (the Ten Commandments above all) but to 'perfect' them, to raise the standards even higher. Jesus himself is the perfect embodiment of someone living the beatitudes.

Fifth Sunday in Ordinary Time • Year A

Collect

The prayer asks for God's care and protection so that, in all matters, we may be kept safe.

First Reading   Isaiah 58:7-10

Today's reading from the prophecy of Deutero-Isaiah urges us to be generous in our attention to the poor. God will reward our kindness to those in need.

Psalm 111 (112)

The good man is a light in the darkness for the upright.

A psalm which praises those who are generous to the poor.

Second Reading   1 Corinthians 2:1-5

St Paul continues the theme of last Sunday. His teaching (both in manner and content) comes not from his own ability and wisdom but from the power of the Holy Spirit of God.

Gospel   Matthew 5:13-16

The Sermon on the Mount is a collection, made by the evangelist, of various discourses and sayings of Jesus. Today, it proceeds with Jesus using two metaphors to describe what his followers should be: salt of the earth, light of the world. To remain 'salty' and not become tasteless, the important thing is not being always busy, but that our activity should be born of our love of God and of his power within us. To be the light of the world needs witness that is courageous, genuine and correct.

Sixth Sunday in Ordinary Time • Year A

Collect

We ask God to make our hearts fit places for him to dwell in.

First Reading   Ecclesiasticus 15:15-20

From the Old Testament book of Ecclesiasticus, written in the second century BC by a zealous scribe to uphold Jewish traditions against the hellenisation (imitating Greek culture) which was becoming more widespread.

Today's passage speaks of our free will, especially the choice between right and wrong. But it is God's will that we should always choose the former.

Psalm 118 (119)

They are happy who follow God's law!

Some verses extracted from the longest psalm: 176 verses. We pray for obedience to God's precepts.

Second Reading   1 Corinthians 2:6-10

As last Sunday, St Paul asserts that Christians have a wisdom that comes only from God and by which we know what God reveals through the Spirit.

Gospel   Matthew 5:17-37

Continuing the teaching of Jesus which Matthew gathers in the Sermon on the Mount, today's extract recounts that Christ declares that he does not abolish the precepts of the Old Testament. His teaching perfects and fulfils them in the sense that he raises those laws to a new and higher form to conform to the values of the kingdom he has come to inaugurate. Jesus illustrates this with examples; four are in today's gospel and two in next week's.

Seventh Sunday in Ordinary Time • Year A

Collect

A straightforward prayer in which we ask God that all that we say and do may be pleasing to him.

First Reading   Leviticus 19:1-2.17-18

From the book of Leviticus, the third book of the Pentateuch and which, interrupting the narrative of God's chosen people, is devoted to the promulgation of laws and precepts. In today's reading, God instructs Moses to tell the Israelites to be holy. Specifically, they are to treat others with honesty and kindness. 'You must love your neighbour as yourself.'

Psalm 102 (103)

The Lord is compassion and love.

This psalm begins with a call to praise God and then provides the motive for this praise: God is totally merciful; he forgives us, heals us, redeems us.

Second Reading   **1 Corinthians 3:16-23**

God lives in us, making us a sacred place. Paul then repeats what he has already said: our knowledge of the faith seems human foolishness but it is the wisdom of God.

Gospel   **Matthew 5:38-48**

We continue to read from that part of St Matthew's Gospel called the Sermon on the Mount. Specifically, today's subject is the continuation and conclusion of last week's: Jesus proclaims that he has come not to abolish the Law and prophecies of the Old Testament, but to bring that teaching to perfection. 'You must be perfect as your heavenly Father is perfect'.

Today's passage gives two examples: first, when others demand or ask something of you, give even more than they demand or ask; and second, our love for others must include our enemies as well as our friends.

[Note that 'It was said ... hate your enemy' is not a reference to any Old Testament law from God; it may have been a slogan of some people in the past or else an inaccurate rendering of 'there is less obligation to love your enemy than your friend'.]

Eighth Sunday in Ordinary Time • Year A

Collect

A prayer for God's peace throughout the world. In particular, may the Church enjoy that gift.

First Reading   **Isaiah 49:14-15**

In the prophecy of Deutero-Isaiah, God firmly declares his unconditional fidelity to his people.

Psalm 61 (62)

In God alone is my soul at rest.

Words of trust to respond to God's assurance in the first reading.

Second Reading   **1 Corinthians 4:1-5**

In chapter 4 of 1st Corinthians (and the final extract from that letter of St Paul at present), we are told that we are Christ's servants, entrusted with continuing his teaching. God alone is the judge of our fidelity to that mission.

Gospel   Matthew 6:24-34

In today's extract from the Sermon on the Mount (from Matthew, chapter 6), Jesus tells us of the basic choice we have to make: either God or material wealth. He goes on to assure us that, if we opt for the former, God will ensure that our material needs are met. (The final sentence of today's gospel is not part of Jesus' teaching but a later and irrelevant addition, perhaps a local proverb.)

Ninth Sunday in Ordinary Time • Year A

Collect

We ask God, in his providence, to grant us what will be for our benefit and to keep from us whatever may harm us.

First Reading   Deuteronomy 11:18.26-28.32

In the book of Deuteronomy, there are long discourses of Moses to the Jews while on their way to the Promised Land. One discourse is on the basic principles of the God-given Law. This extract is from the conclusion of that discourse. Moses insists that the people must faithfully observe all the laws. They are to have them written and worn on their hands and foreheads (and – though not in today's reading – to be taught to their children and written on the doorposts of their houses).

Psalm 30 (31)

Be a rock of refuge for me, O Lord.

This psalm is a prayer to God in time of trial.

Second Reading   Romans 3:21-25.28

We begin a long series of sixteen weeks with readings from St Paul's letter to the church in Rome. In this reading, Paul teaches that God's promise to save his people (which is 'God's justice'), hitherto known only through the Old Testament and therefore for Jews, has now been revealed through Jesus Christ. It is a free gift offered to everyone, and acquired through faith in Christ our Saviour and not through the Old Testament Law.

Gospel   Matthew 7:21-27

In the final piece of Matthew's gospel presented as Our Lord's Sermon on the Mount, Jesus describes the true disciple. It is not someone who seems to do great things, but the person who listens to the Lord's teaching and puts it into practice, and thus does the will of the Father.

Tenth Sunday in Ordinary Time • Year A

Collect

We pray that God, the source of all that is good, may guide us to discern and do what is right.

First Reading   Hosea 6:3-6

The prophet Hosea (8th century BC) lived in very troubled times in Israel. Assyria threatened to invade, several kings were assassinated in rebellions and moral and religious corruption was widespread. In today's extract, Hosea tells the people that God's judgment on them is certain. Speaking in God's name, the prophet severely scolds the people; their repentance was shallow, they deserve God's anger.

Psalm 49 (50)

I will show God's salvation to the upright.

In the psalm God comes to judge Israel and rejects sacrifice if it is not sincere and if offered by people with contempt for the commandments. However, today we use verses of the psalm in which this anger of God is much less evident. He welcomes sincere offerings and promises his help when asked for it.

Second Reading   Romans 4:18-25

We continue to read from St Paul to the Romans. The apostle tells us that Abraham was a man of faith and hope who, though it seemed impossible, believed and trusted God's promise that he would have descendants; Abraham was justified, made righteous by his faith. Similarly, we shall be justified if we have faith in God who raised Jesus from the dead.

Gospel   Matthew 9:9-13

Jesus calls a tax collector to be one of his disciples. He is named Matthew (here, in the gospel according to Matthew; but in the other two synoptic gospels his name is given as Levi). Jesus has a meal with him and other tax collectors, a fact which some pharisees criticise since tax collectors were extortioners and collaborators with the foreign power and therefore regarded as ritually unclean. Jesus' reply is typical of him and illustrates the essential character of his ministry.

Eleventh Sunday in Ordinary Time • Year A

Collect

Admitting our inability to do anything good without God's help, we ask for the grace to be obedient in both intention and deed.

First Reading   Exodus 19:2-6

The Israelites, in this passage of the Book of Exodus, are in the Sinai wilderness. Moses climbs Mount Sinai (also known as Mount Horeb), called by God, who then promises that he will make a covenant with the people of Israel; they will be a kingdom of priests, a consecrated nation. (In the New Testament, these phrases are used of us, Christians, as a result of the new covenant sealed by the blood of Christ: see 1st Peter 2:9).

Psalm 99 (100)

We are his people, the sheep of his flock.

This short psalm is a call to praise God willingly because of his love for us.

Second Reading   Romans 5:6-11

In today's excerpt from the letter to the Romans, St Paul argues that, since by Christ's death we have been reconciled to God, justified and made righteous, we can be assured of salvation by the God who loves us.

Gospel   Matthew 9:36-10:8

Several points are threaded together in today's gospel. Jesus laments that, although there were so many who wanted to hear the Good News, so few were able to give it. He feels compassion for the people, 'harassed and dejected'. So the gospel then names the twelve men whom he had chosen from among his disciples to be apostles and recounts his instructions to them regarding their mission of preaching and healing. They are to go only to Jewish areas; this restriction is due to the fact that, as descendants of the chosen people, Jews are the first to hear God's plan for his Son.

Twelfth Sunday in Ordinary Time • Year A

Collect

Confident of God's continuing guidance, we pray that we may always live lives faithful to him.

First Reading   Jeremiah 20:10-13

From the prophecy of Jeremiah, a good and holy man living in Jerusalem in very troubled times. The extract is from the end of the sixth century BC. The prophet speaks of his enemies who want to harm him, but he expresses his trust in God for his deliverance.

Psalm 68 (69)

In your great love, answer me, O God.

The psalm is a lament for suffering. The chosen verses speak of someone suffering because of his fidelity to God; he calls upon God to help him and those who suffer with him. The psalm is considered by Christians as messianic and is quoted in the New Testament.

Second Reading   Romans 5:12-15

Today's extract from St Paul's letter to the Romans follows immediately after last week's. It states the doctrine of original sin. St Paul teaches that, since death is the punishment for sin and entered the world because of Adam's sin, we can conclude, from the fact that death awaits us all, that sin entered us all through that first fall (which, of course, preceded the Law which God gave to Moses).

St Paul then draws the parallel with Christ, 'although the gift...outweighed the fall'.

The phrase 'because everyone has sinned' (verse 12) is ambiguous; either 'all share in Adam's sin' or 'by our own personal sins'.

Gospel   Matthew 10:26-33

Having chosen 'the Twelve', Jesus instructs them in their mission, to be carried out especially after his ascension. Despite hostility, they are to be fearless and to proclaim Christ's teaching in its fullness. He will be their witness to his Father.

Thirteenth Sunday in Ordinary Time • Year A

Collect

We pray that God, our Father by adoption, may keep us from the darkness of error and ensure that we always walk in the light of truth.

First Reading   2 Kings 4:8-11.14-16

This is a story about Elisha in the second book of the Kings. The period is mid-9th century BC. Elisha, formerly the assistant of the prophet Elijah, is now his successor. Shunem is a Palestinian town. The woman and her husband show kindness to Elisha and his servant Gehazi. The couple are childless and, to reward their thoughtfulness, Elisha promises that, though old, they will have a son the following year.

Psalm 88 (89)

I will sing for ever of your love, O Lord.

The psalm is a hymn in praise of God's faithful love for his people.

Second Reading   Romans 6:3-4.8-11

We continue with passages from the letter to the Romans. Faith and baptism are two essentials in our being made righteous. Hence St Paul sees a parallel between Christ, dead and buried in the tomb and then raised to new and immortal life, and us, dead to sin and plunged (in those early days, immersed) into the 'tomb' of the baptismal font and then raised up to new life with death and sin conquered.

Gospel   Matthew 10:37-42

Our Lord's instruction of the twelve chosen to be apostles is continued from last week and concluded in this passage from Matthew's gospel. Two points are made: a disciple of Christ must give up all normal attachments; and a disciple of Christ has a right to be welcomed and cared for by those he seeks to serve.

Fourteenth Sunday in Ordinary Time • Year A

Collect

Recognising that our fallen world was raised up through Christ's humble acceptance of suffering, we pray that we may experience the lasting joy that our rescue from sin brings us.

First Reading   Zechariah 9:9-10

The book of Zechariah has two parts, the earlier dating from the late 6th century BC, the other from the late 4th century. Today's reading is from the second part and speaks of the expectation of a humble messiah (hence Palm

Sunday and Jesus riding on a donkey) but one who will bring peace to Israel and to the world.

Psalm 144 (145)

I will bless your name for ever,
O God my King. or *Alleluia!*

We praise and thank God the King, who is infinitely merciful.

Second Reading   Romans 8:9.11-13

We continue reading from St Paul's letter to the Christians at Rome, this week from chapter 8. It speaks of the difference between the Old Testament (or Mosaic) Law which cannot of itself bring us salvation, and Christ who by the Spirit given to us can destroy sin in us. The Spirit raised Jesus from the dead and so also gives life to us, putting an end to sin by which we would die.

Gospel   Matthew 11:25-30

For the previous three Sundays of Matthew's gospel, Jesus has been with the Twelve. Today, after preaching to the people in general, he gives expression to his thoughts about his message. It is a message whose content is common to both Father and Son, it is for ordinary people, not the learned, and its demands will bring us peace and happiness.

Fifteenth Sunday in Ordinary Time • Year A

Collect

The light which God gives maintains us in the truth or restores us to it; so we pray that, by God's help, all Christians may remain faithful to Christ and his teaching.

First Reading   Isaiah 55:10-11

It is useful to say a little about the Book of Isaiah. The first 39 chapters are by Isaiah who lived in the 8th century BC when Israel was weak and vulnerable to neighbouring powers. The chapters from 40 to 55 seem to belong to the 6th century BC when Israel, and specifically Judah, was in exile in Babylon; the author then would be perhaps a disciple of Isaiah (and therefore designated by posterity as Deutero-Isaiah). The final eleven chapters appear to be a mixture of themes from pre-exilic, exilic and post-exilic times, written by followers of Isaiah.

Today's extract is from chapter 55, at the very end of the second part of the book. It is an assurance that, just as the varieties of weather sent by God infallibly achieve their effect on our crops, so God's word is similarly unfailingly effective. ('God's word'? The teaching or the Son? Some scholars see this text as a possible source of the theology of the Word in John's gospel.)

Psalm 64 (65)

Some seed fell into rich soil
and produced its crop.

The people thank God for sending rain in abundance. The verses used describe springtime in Judah.

Second Reading   Romans 8:18-23

In this week's extract from the letter to the Romans, St Paul teaches that, as coheirs with Christ, we, and indeed all creation, await our being able to share in God's glory. It is sin, and God's punishment for sin, that meanwhile delays this fulfilment of our destiny. This passage has ecological significance.

Gospel   Matthew 13:1-23

The parable of the sower is an explanation of the various ways in which different people receive Christ's teaching concerning God's eternal plan of salvation for us. Some people accept the teaching and act on it, others, for various reasons, fail to do so. The examples of the various ways would resonate with peasants and their experience of work in their own fields.

Jesus preferred to use parables for teaching. There are about forty parables in the gospels. But why did he often not explain the parables to the people, but only to his close disciples? A difficult question. Probably a way of saying that most Jews did not accept Jesus' proclamation of the kingdom – or did not accept those whom Jesus appointed to continue the proclamation. In that case, therefore, even the benefits they enjoyed under the Old Covenant will no longer be available to them when the New Covenant is inaugurated (13:12 '...even what he has will be taken away'). Another explanation of these difficult words may be that, for those who choose not to follow Jesus, even the little of his teaching they heard will soon be lost. The verses about the closed or shallow hearts (quoting Isaiah 6:9-10) may be a later insertion in the light of events.

Sixteenth Sunday in Ordinary Time • Year A

Collect

Asking God to be generous with his gifts and graces, we pray that, with faith, hope and love, we may be more ready to obey him.

First Reading   Wisdom 12:13.16-19

This reading is from the book of Wisdom, written in the 1st century BC in Greek by an unidentified Jewish sage of Alexandria (attributed to Solomon but only in homage). The book speaks of the origin, nature and function of wisdom. In today's passage, God is shown to have all the qualities of wisdom, especially in his way of treating others, including those who have offended; he is an example for us all to follow.

Psalm 85 (86)

O Lord, you are good and forgiving.

The extract praises God's goodness, and in particular his mercy and readiness to forgive.

Second Reading   Romans 8:26-27

In last week's excerpt from the letter to the Romans, St Paul spoke of the delay before we attain our full destiny. This week we are told of the need for constant prayer. It can be difficult for us to find words for prayer so the Holy Spirit 'expresses our plea in a way which could never be put into words'. So prayer need not always be in words. In addition to mental prayer, prayer can also be in sound but without words. St Augustine likens the experience to a mother whose love for her baby is expressed in audible, but wordless, lullaby; our love for God can be similarly expressed when words are unnecessary.

Gospel   Matthew 13:24-43

Chapter 13 of Matthew's gospel collects a number of Christ's parables which probably were spoken on different occasions. As with last week (the parable of the sower), Jesus reserves the explanation of the parables for the apostles, perhaps a way of suggesting that the crowds were undecided, even reluctant, about accepting the teaching of Jesus.

Today's passage has three parables. First, the parable of the wheat and the darnel: the unwanted weed is not torn up at once, but left until the harvest of the wheat; similarly with evil people on earth. The second and third parables are of the mustard seed and the yeast: both seem insignificant at the start but, in practice, have huge increases and results. In like manner, the kingdom which Jesus inaugurated seems unpretentious at first, but is destined for great growth and effect.

Seventeenth Sunday in Ordinary Time • Year A

Collect

We seek God's protection and his guidance to use wisely the things of this world as helps to cling to the things that last.

First Reading   1 Kings 3:5.7-12

As Solomon (in 970 BC) succeeds his father King David and begins his reign of forty years, God offers him the choice of a gift. He asks for the gift of wisdom to be a good leader of his people. God is pleased with his choice and gladly promises to grant his request.

Psalm 118 (119)

Lord, how I love your law!

This is the longest of all the psalms (176 verses). It praises God's Law, in the sense of all God's teaching. We use verses which speak of the love and esteem that we have for God's Law and of our desire to obey it.

Second Reading   Romans 8:28-30

The passage from the letter to the Romans continues in chapter 8 and follows immediately the passage that was last Sunday's second reading. God's plan means that, by the conquest of sin and our justification through Christ, those called by God become images of his Son and indeed his brothers and sisters. Through faith and baptism we are to share the glory of God.

Gospel   Matthew 13:44-52

This is the final batch of parables from chapter 13 of St Matthew's gospel. The parables of the finding of a treasure and a fine pearl teach that, to gain God's kingdom, we must leave all earthly things; but such renunciation is well worth doing; it is life-changing. The parable of the dragnet has its own explanation in the text. The final sentence of today's gospel passage refers to anyone who, if already a Jewish teacher, then becomes a disciple of Jesus – that person will have access to the wisdom of both Old and New Testaments.

Eighteenth Sunday in Ordinary Time • Year A

Collect

With loving trust we ask God to repair what has been damaged of his creation and to save it from further harm.

First Reading   Isaiah 55:1-3

Today's reading is from Deutero-Isaiah, chapter 55, and therefore the final chapter of the second part of the book, towards the end of the Babylonian exile (see p.73). God will provide spiritual nourishment without cost to those who are penniless. The reading ends with the promise of a covenant that will last for ever, a promise which Christians see fulfilled in Christ and sealed by the shedding of his blood.

Psalm 144 (145)

You open wide your hand, O Lord,
you grant our desires.

God is gentle, loving, compassionate, generous in meeting all our needs.

Second Reading   Romans 8:35.37-39

Chapter 8 of the letter to the Romans closes with a stirring hymn of praise and thanksgiving to God. St Paul starts by asking: 'After saying this, what can we add?' and then proceeds to write the words which cannot fail to arouse our faith and hope in the God who loves us. (It is a pity that today's reading does not begin from verse 31!)

Gospel   Matthew 14:13-21

Today's gospel shows us again how Jesus exercised his public ministry through teaching and acts of compassion. In this account of the first miracle of feeding the multitude, the words 'Give them something to eat yourselves' are important. Our initial response when we hear of people in need can be very selfish – they should be able to look after themselves, buying food (whereas Jesus' response is for them to be given food). In addition to its eucharistic prefiguring, the episode is also relevant for today: those who have plenty of food and those who are hungry. The miracle teaches us that, even today, if we share what we have, there will be enough for everyone. Are we genuine disciples if we ignore or reject the lesson?

Nineteenth Sunday in Ordinary Time • Year A

Collect

Since the Holy Spirit assures us that we are adopted children of God, we pray that we may learn how to live out that privilege and reach our inheritance of eternal life.

First Reading   1 Kings 19:9.11-13

In the first book of the Kings, we read about the successors of King David and his son Solomon. In the ninth century BC, Ahab (king of the northern kingdom of Israel) and his wife Jezebel want to kill the prophet Elijah who has condemned them and the prophets of Baal for idolatry. Elijah seeks refuge by hiding in a cave. God calls him to meet him. Elijah obeys and finds that God is not in the storm, the earthquake or the lightning but in a gentle breeze. God tells him to go to Syria to anoint a king who would slaughter the Israelite idolaters; Elijah is also to anoint Elisha as his own disciple and successor.

[God in the gentle breeze may signify God's will that the fiery Elijah should copy God's calmer way of confronting people or, a slightly different explanation, that God is a spirit and instructs his prophets in an intimate manner.]

Psalm 84 (85)

Let us see, O Lord, your mercy
and give us your saving help.

This psalm is for the exiles returned to their own land of Israel. There God will bestow peace, justice, mercy and prosperity – promises to be fulfilled in the time of the messiah.

Second Reading   Romans 9:1-5

Having taught in previous chapters of his letter to the Romans that salvation comes through the Holy Spirit and by faith, St Paul, in chapters 9 to 11 and beginning today, confronts the problem of Israel, the people who received the promise of salvation but who, for the most part, do not believe in Christ.

The final sentence of today's reading has an unusual ending for St Paul, a doxology addressed to Christ as God. Normally, St Paul speaks of Christ as subordinate to the Father, as God made man and acting as the Father's agent in the work of salvation.

Gospel Matthew 14:22-33

The event in today's gospel follows on immediately after the feeding of the multitude (last Sunday's passage). The fear of the disciples with Jesus not present and their lack of faith is a symbol of the early Church – the boat, beset from within by fear and little faith, threatened from outside by hostility. It is also symbolic of the Church today. Fear is the great obstacle, the reason for our lack of faith and of our difficulty in knowing, loving and following Jesus. It is not easy to rid ourselves of fear.

Twentieth Sunday in Ordinary Time • Year A

Collect

We ask God, by his own love, to bring us to love him above everything else so that we may reach the inheritance with him that he has promised.

First Reading Isaiah 56:1.6-7

This reading is the opening of the third part of the book of Isaiah and is written after the return from exile in Babylon. The passage has a broad outlook – foreigners should be admitted into the Jewish community, provided they observe the required ritual practices.

Psalm 66 (67)

Let the peoples praise you, O God;
let all the peoples praise you.

This short psalm was probably sung at the harvest festival. It invites even the pagan nations to serve the one God.

Second Reading Romans 11:13-15.29-32

St Paul continues his thoughts about the Jews who have rejected Christ. He sees this rejection as having been the opportunity for the 'pagans' (that is, the gentiles) to have been evangelised. He is God's agent for this, though he regrets the Jews' refusal and looks forward to a day when they will have faith in Christ. He calls a conversion of the Jews 'nothing less than a resurrection from the dead'. The meaning of this phrase is disputed: either 'a great favour from God comparable to the final resurrection' or 'a cause of great utility and joy for gentiles' or 'for Jews a transition from death to life'.

Gospel   Matthew 15:21-28

This reading from St Matthew refers to the healing of a Canaanite woman's daughter. Jesus is probably in the Jewish south of the region, the woman (Canaanite = Syro-Phoenician) is a gentile from further north. Jesus makes it clear that, for him personally, his mission is to Jews; for him, contact with gentiles is an exception. The words of Jesus to the woman seem very insulting to us; even in Palestine at that time, they are somewhat harsh. But commentators explain that such tit-for-tat exchanges of wit or insult were (and still are) common in the Middle East.

Notice that, despite the exchanges, neither the woman nor Jesus accept the marginalisation or abandonment or neglect of women and their rights or needs.

Twenty-First Sunday in Ordinary Time
• Year A

Collect

We ask God to make us so obedient to him and so full of hope that, in this changing world, we may be intent on reaching the place of true happiness.

First Reading   Isaiah 22:19-23

This passage from 'First' Isaiah (see p.73) probably is dated 705 BC. The Jews were celebrating a victory over allies of Assyria but Isaiah rebukes them in God's name because the victory is soon to be followed by complete defeat and exile. In particular, Shebna, King Hezekiah's major-domo, is dismissed for enriching himself, and especially for constructing an expensive tomb for himself. Eliakim is named to succeed him.

Psalm 137 (138)

Your love, O Lord, is eternal,
discard not the work of your hands.

This psalm is a hymn of thanksgiving to God for his kindness.

Second Reading   Romans 11:33-36

Immediately after his thoughts about God's plan to save both Jews and gentiles which we read last week (Romans 11), St Paul breaks into this hymn of praise to God's wisdom and mercy. (The three questions in the passage are a quotation from Isaiah, chapter 40, verses 13 and 14.)

Gospel   Matthew 16:13-20

This is a key passage in the public ministry of Jesus and the relationship between him and his closest disciples. It is the moment when Jesus requires a declaration of faith that they believe him to be the messiah (in all three synoptic gospels) and the Son of God (only in Matthew). Furthermore, it is the occasion on which the apostles make a binding commitment of fidelity to Jesus and what he demands of them.

The name 'Peter' was apparently not used either in Greek or in Aramaic as a personal name until Jesus gave it to Simon.

'I will build my Church'. The word, which means an assembly, was used in the Old Testament for the community of God's Chosen People. By using the term (along with 'the kingdom of heaven'), Jesus shows that his followers here on earth were to be an organised society.

The 'power of the keys to bind and loose' is primarily disciplinary and secondarily doctrinal and juridical (decisions on faith and morals).

Twenty-Second Sunday in Ordinary Time
• Year A

Collect

We ask God, from whom we receive everything good, to help us love him more, to increase his gifts in us and to protect them with his care.

First Reading   Jeremiah 20:7-9

The prophet Jeremiah, who lived in Jerusalem in the seventh and early sixth centuries BC and at a time when the city was besieged and captured by King Nebuchadnezzar and the Chaldaeans, speaks his thoughts to God. When he spoke God's message to the people, he was insulted and derided; he wanted to abandon his mission, but Jeremiah says that he could not because God had seduced and overpowered him.

Psalm 62 (63)

> *For you my soul is thirsting,*
> *O Lord my God.*

A psalm that expresses deep longing for God and his loving help. It is attributed to King David when in the Judean wilderness.

Second Reading   Romans 12:1-2

Nearing the end of his letter to the church in Rome, St Paul (chapters 12-15) exhorts them to remain faithful to God, to live in a way that is pleasing to God and thus to discover God's will for them.

Gospel   Matthew 16:21-27

After the events recounted last Sunday, Jesus at once tells his disciples of God's plan for him – Jerusalem, passion, death and resurrection. Peter is severely rebuked for his misguided attempt to deter Jesus from this plan. Peter must learn that Jesus is not only the victorious messiah but also 'the suffering servant' (as in Isaiah). The final sentence today is from a different occasion but has some relevance to the subject of the rest of the passage.

Twenty-Third Sunday in Ordinary Time
• Year A

Collect

We ask God to grant us, his adopted family, that, believing in Christ, we may be truly free and reach our promised inheritance.

First Reading   Ezekiel 33:7-9

The prophet Ezekiel lived among the Jewish exiles in Babylon in the first decades of the sixth century BC. His writings are sometimes reproachful and threatening, sometimes comforting and promising. In today's extract, God is giving Ezekiel his instructions about his prophetic mission.

Psalm 94 (95)

> *O that today you would listen to his voice!*
> *Harden not your hearts.*

The psalm is a call urging us to come to God and to pray. It is used as the opening of each day's Divine Office.

[Meribah and Massah recall the incident of the Jews in the wilderness where, in reply to their complaints about having no water to drink, God told Moses to strike the rock and then water gushed out of it. 'Meribah' means dispute, 'Massah' means temptation (Exodus 17:1-7).]

Second Reading   Romans 13:8-10

Another extract from the exhortation towards the end of the letter to the Romans. Love is the law in all its fullness and completeness.

Gospel   Matthew 18:15-20

Chapter 18 of St Matthew's gospel has a number of sayings and instructions of Jesus to his disciples. We hear three of them today: how to correct wrongdoers in the community; the extension to the Church's ministers of the power of binding and loosing (in matters of faith, morals and discipline); and the efficacy of prayer in common since, in that case, Jesus will be present there.

Twenty-Fourth Sunday in Ordinary Time
• Year A

Collect

We ask God, our creator and ruler, to help us experience his mercy and willingly serve him.

First Reading   Ecclesiasticus 27:30-28:7

The book called Ecclesiasticus was written by a Jewish sage known as Ben Sira. It dates from the second century BC when the Jews were being influenced by the pagan culture of hellenism. In this extract, the author is giving advice on morality and, specifically, on avoiding resentment and thoughts of vengeance if one expects God to show compassion and pardon to us.

Psalm 102 (103)

> *The Lord is compassion and love,*
> *slow to anger and rich in mercy.*

This psalm echoes the first reading and extols the qualities of God which were revealed to Moses.

Second Reading   Romans 14:7-9

In this last extract from St Paul's letter to the Christians of Rome, he speaks of Christ who, through his death and resurrection, has become Lord of all of us, whether we are alive or dead.

Gospel   Matthew 18:21-35

Jesus teaches the duty of continued and unending forgiveness of wrongdoers (77 or 70 x 7 times?) and illustrates his teaching with a parable. (10,000 talents is a huge sum, 100 denarii is paltry.) Yet this is a strange parable to illustrate the teaching, which is that forgiveness should be normal, not heroic and spectacular. Yet the servant does not forgive the small debtor, the other servants do not forgive their fellow servant and, finally, neither does the king! Perhaps the real lesson is merely this, that if we do not forgive hurts etc. which are trivial, can we expect God to forgive us our sins, which are serious?

Twenty-Fifth Sunday in Ordinary Time
• Year A

Collect

Since the basis of all God's commandments is love of him and of our neighbours, we ask for the grace to obey the commandments and so reach eternal life.

First Reading   Isaiah 55:6-9

Near the end of the second part of Isaiah (6th century BC), and towards the end of the captivity in Babylon, the prophet urges his readers to return to the Lord, to be converted. He stresses how different are God's standards from ours.

Psalm 144 (145)

The Lord is close to all who call him.

A hymn of praise to God, the good and merciful king.

Second Reading   Philippians 1:20-24.27

For the next four Sundays, the reading is from Paul's letter to the Christians of Philippi on the northern coast of Greece. The letter is friendly and with advice rather than doctrinal teaching; probably written 56/57 when Paul seems to have been 'in chains', perhaps at Ephesus. He speaks of his closeness to Christ, his union with him, which he longs to make even closer – but God seems to want him to remain on earth and continue his mission for the time being.

Gospel
Matthew 20:1-16

The parable of the labourers in the vineyard is a teaching on God's gift to us of eternal life. God is generous to all, unjust to none; eternal life is a promise and a gift, not dependent on how long we live and work on earth. The parable can be shocking and seem very unfair yet, in a somewhat similar way, Jesus associated mainly with the disreputable and not the pious and meritorious.

Twenty-Sixth Sunday in Ordinary Time
• Year A

Collect

Acknowledging God's infinite mercy, we pray for the grace to inherit his promises of eternal life.

First Reading
Ezekiel 18:25-28

The prophet Ezekiel was active in the sixth century BC, teaching the exiles in Babylon. In chapter 18, on our individual moral responsibility, God refutes any accusation, in today's reading, that he is unjust; rather, if a just man turns to evil, he will be punished, and if an evil man renounces sin, he will have life.

Psalm 24 (25)

Remember your mercy, Lord.

Today's selected psalm verses are an appropriate response to the first reading, although the full psalm prays for God's protection at a time of danger.

Second Reading
Philippians 2:1-11

Writing to the Philippians, St Paul pleads for unity among the Christians of the town. To achieve this, they must be humble, self-effacing, unselfish and thoughtful of others. To provide the exemplar and model to follow, St Paul (in chapter 2, verses 6-11) quotes a hymn of the early Church: Christ undergoes a double kenosis (self-emptying – retaining his divine nature but not evidently, he assumes human form and is executed as a criminal); but, after his self-sacrifice, God ensures that he is recognised as God and is given the divine title of *Kyrios* (Lord).

Gospel   Matthew 21:28-32

The parable of the two sons illustrates the teaching of the first reading and is verified in the two reactions to the preaching of John the Baptist. Jesus speaks very harshly to the religious leaders but the message is simple: with God, it is not our talk that matters, but our deeds.

Twenty-Seventh Sunday in Ordinary Time
• Year A

Collect

To God, whose kindness is far beyond our expectations, we pray for forgiveness and for the gifts that only he can know and bestow.

First Reading   Isaiah 5:1-7

The reading comes in the first part of Isaiah, when Israel is threatened by stronger neighbours. The passage is called 'the song of the vineyard'.

It is a poem composed by the prophet and it describes Israel as a vine, carefully tended by the vineyard owner but, because it produced only sour grapes, he rejects it.

Similar images of Israel as a vine which disappoints the owner are found in Jeremiah and Ezekiel.

Psalm 79 (80)

> *The vineyard of the Lord*
> *is the House of Israel.*

The psalm laments the fate of Israel, conquered by enemies, and begs God to restore its freedom and prosperity. Vv. 8-15 and 18-19 (used today) have the image of a vine, asking God to come to the rescue and promising fidelity in the future.

Second Reading   Philippians 4:6-9

St Paul offers advice and encouragement to the Christians of Philippi. God will answer their prayers and will give them his gift of true peace. Paul urges his readers to persevere in living a good life, following his example and teaching.

Gospel   Matthew 21:33-43

This is the parable of the wicked husbandmen in which Jesus portrays Israel

86

as a vineyard, cherished by its owner. But the story has more detail than today's first reading since the prophets, Jesus himself, Jews and gentiles (respectively, the owner's servants, his son, the original and later tenants) are all brought into the lesson. Jesus is talking to the religious leaders of the Jews, the very people who are the guilty ones. Of course, the parable has relevance for us: God does not want a sterile Christianity from which the desired fruit is not forthcoming.

Twenty-Eighth Sunday in Ordinary Time
• Year A

Collect

We ask for God's grace to be always with us, urging us to help others.

First Reading   Isaiah 25:6-10

In Isaiah, chapters 24 to 27 are a vision of the end times and God's final judgment. The descriptions are poetic and apocalyptic. Chapter 25 (today's reading) speaks of the comforting aspect of the end times, using the image of a messianic banquet for all peoples on Mount Sion (Jerusalem).

Psalm 22 (23)

In the Lord's own house shall I dwell
for ever and ever.

Today's responsorial psalm uses the entire text of Psalm 22 (23). God's care for us is presented in two images, first as a shepherd and then as hosting a messianic banquet.

Second Reading   Philippians 4:12-14.19-20

In this fourth and final extract from his letter to his beloved Philippians, Paul speaks of the ability God has given him to cope with any conditions.

Nonetheless, he is grateful for the help he has received and assures them of God's loving kindness.

Gospel   Matthew 22:1-14

Today's parable of the wedding feast bears some similarities to last Sunday's (the wicked husbandmen) and, of course, to today's first reading. In the gospel, those who refuse the invitation are the Jews (the destruction of Jerusalem in 70 AD is foretold). The guest ejected had arrived without the 'wedding garment' of good works. The final sentence ('Many are called, but few are chosen') refers to the first part of the parable and to the Jews, some of whom are among 'the chosen'.

The parable, of course, has the contemporary lesson that those declining the invitation may be seen as coming from among ourselves.

Twenty-Ninth Sunday in Ordinary Time
• Year A

Collect

We ask God that we may always do his will and serve him sincerely.

First Reading   Isaiah 45:1.4-6

In the sixth century BC Cyrus the Great, founder of the Persian Empire, invaded and conquered Babylon and freed the Jews held captive there, allowing them to return to Israel in 538 BC (see p.11). Deutero-Isaiah (see p.73) sees him as God's anointed instrument, as in today's extract.

Psalm 95 (96)

Give the Lord glory and power.

This is a psalm which praises God for his great glory. He is the universal king and all peoples should worship him.

Second Reading   1 Thessalonians 1:1-5

St Paul visited Thessalonika (a city on the north-east coast of Greece; today Thessaloniki) in summer of the year 50 and wrote two letters to the Christians there some months afterwards. These are his first letters, the earliest of the thirteen that we have. One of their main themes is the 'parousia', the end times; and the impression is given that Paul expected the second coming of Christ to be imminent. [The Greek word parousia, meaning 'presence', was used by early Christians for the second coming of Jesus and the other anticipated events associated with it.]

For five Sundays, starting today, we shall hear passages from the first letter to the Thessalonians. Today we have the opening remarks in which Paul praises the Christian community in the city for their faith, hope and love.

Gospel   Matthew 22:15-21

This gospel passage on paying tribute to the Roman emperor needs careful explanation. The party of the pharisees resented the Roman occupation (but were against the use of force to oppose it) while the Herodians, supporters of the Herodian dynasty, were fervent supporters of the Romans (on whom their position depended). The group try to flatter Jesus and to embarrass him but, to their question, he gives no direct answer. His answer is merely 'this coin has Caesar's head on it so it must be his; give Caesar back what belongs to him'. The words of Jesus assert merely the de facto existence of Roman power and property in Palestine, not its right to exist there. The incident is found also in Mark (12:13-17) and Luke (20:20-26).

Thirtieth Sunday in Ordinary Time • Year A

Collect

Asking God to increase our faith, hope and love, we also pray to be obedient to him so as to receive what he has promised.

First Reading   Exodus 22:20-26

The book of Exodus tells us that, after giving the Ten Commandments to Moses (for the guidance of the Israelites), God then elaborates the various commandments in great detail. Today's extract speaks of the moral duty of treating various vulnerable people with consideration and kindness.

Psalm 17 (18)

I love you, Lord, my strength.

This psalm praises God for his protection of the king and specifically of David, in danger from Saul and other enemies. The verses in today's liturgy can be used to thank God for his protection of any who are in danger.

Second Reading   1 Thessalonians 1:5-10

In this second of five extracts from his first letter to the Thessalonians, St Paul congratulates the Christian community in the city. They have followed his example and, despite opposition, have themselves become an example to other parts of Greece. St Paul mentions that he has no need to tell others of the Thessalonians' faith and good conduct; others have already told him about them.

Gospel   Matthew 22:34-40

There are over 600 precepts in the Mosaic Law, which helps explain the pharisee's question. Jesus retrieves the essential one about love of God above all and unites it with love of neighbours since God loves every human being and therefore to love God and not love our neighbours is not morally possible. All three synoptic gospels recount this incident, but with differences. Luke uses it to introduce the parable of the Good Samaritan, Mark regards the questioner in a favourable light but Matthew speaks of the question being asked 'to disconcert' Jesus. [Matthew generally views the scribes and pharisees in a less friendly way than do the other evangelists. The Sadducees, mentioned at the start of the passage, denied the resurrection of the body because the belief is not found in the Pentateuch.]

Thirty-First Sunday in Ordinary Time
• Year A

Collect

Recognising that even our service of God is his gift, we pray that we may proceed without mishap on the way to receive our promised inheritance.

First Reading   Malachi 1:14-2:2.8-10

The prophet Malachi lived around mid-fifth century BC at a time when a previous era of post-exilic enthusiasm had dwindled and the Jews tended to be religiously lackadaisical. Today's extract shows God's anger with the unfaithful and sinful priests; no wonder the people treat them with contempt. God will visit on the priests the punishment they deserve.

Psalm 130 (131)

Keep my soul in peace before you, O Lord.

This short psalm, used today in its entirety, speaks of the desire to live peacefully and trustfully in God's care.

Second Reading   1 Thessalonians 2:7-9.13

In today's reading from his first letter to the church in Thessalonika, St Paul joyfully recalls his hard but rewarding work among them when he went there to proclaim the gospel. He thanks the Christians of the city for their ready acceptance of his message and their fidelity to it.

Gospel   Matthew 23:1-12

Speaking to his disciples and others listening, Jesus severely criticises the religious leaders of the Jews for their arrogance and their hypocrisy. [A phylactery is a small box or pouch containing within it the most important verses of the Law. It is tied on the forearm or forehead, as prescribed in the Torah. The four tassels were sewn, one at each corner of the cloak. 'Rabbi' is Aramaic for 'my master' and was the usual term for a Jewish teacher.]

The second half of today's gospel seems to be addressed only to the disciples and therefore may well have been spoken on a different occasion.

Matthew's gospel provides some very anti-hierarchical statements and which seem authentically of Jesus; the evangelist may stress them because of some early evidence of aspirations for power among Christians.

Thirty-Second Sunday in Ordinary Time • Year A

Collect

We ask our divine Father to keep us free from all obstacles of mind or body that would hinder us from seeking the things of God.

First Reading   Wisdom 6:12-16

The book of Wisdom was written in Greek by a Jew living in the hellenic culture of Alexandria, probably around 50 BC. The aim of the work is to encourage readers, Jews and gentiles alike, to retain belief in a personal, loving God and not to be distracted by the allure of the surrounding hellenic culture.

Today's extract speaks of wisdom. It is a virtue readily available to all who seek it.

Psalm 62 (63)

> For you my soul is thirsting,
> O God, my God.

The psalm expresses a deep longing for God, our help and whose 'love is better than life'. The responsorial psalm is always a response to the first reading; here, the psalm indicates that wisdom is a divine attribute, even God himself.

Second Reading   1 Thessalonians 4:13-18

St Paul reassures (or enlightens) the Thessalonian Christians that the dead will, like Christ, rise to eternal life. He then states that Christ's teaching (given perhaps in the vision on the way to Damascus, because not in any gospel) is that eternal life will also be given to those still alive at Christ's second coming. By including himself among these latter, he seems to expect that the parousia will not be long delayed.

Gospel   Matthew 25:1-13

The parable of the ten bridesmaids tells of Christians awaiting the second coming of Christ. Even though we do not know when, we must be watchful. The wise course is to live our lives as faithful and sincere disciples of Christ.

Thirty-Third Sunday in Ordinary Time • Year A

Collect

We ask 'the author of all that is good' to give us the happiness of being constant in our service of him.

First Reading   Proverbs 31:10-13.19-20.30-31

The book of Proverbs is a collection of aphorisms and wise sayings, collected over several centuries before Christ and beginning at the time of Solomon (to whom some are attributed) in the tenth century BC. Today's reading, chapter 31, the final chapter in the book, is a poem on the perfect wife, each verse beginning with a consecutive letter of the Hebrew alphabet. Some scholars regard the poem as a description of wisdom personified.

Psalm 127 (128)

O blessed are those who fear the Lord.

The entire psalm is used in today's liturgy. It celebrates the domestic happiness which God gives to good people. 'Your wife like a fruitful vine' responds to the ideal wife of the first reading.

Second Reading   1 Thessalonians 5:1-6

This is the fourth and last extract from 1st Thessalonians. St Paul acknowledges that he does not know when the second coming of Christ will occur. It will come suddenly and when least expected. But, since we are children of light, we must be awake and prepared.

Gospel   Matthew 25:14-30

The parable of the talents reminds us that we share the mission of Jesus for which we receive gifts. These gifts are to be used to build God's kingdom and eventually we must give an account of our use of them. The third servant is motivated neither by love of Christ nor a wish to further his mission but rather by fear, anxious to preserve what he has been given and thus not daring to be creatively faithful.

Our Lord Jesus Christ, King of the Universe
• Year A
(Thirty-Fourth Sunday in Ordinary Time)

Collect

Since it is God's will that everything be restored in his Son, King of the Universe, we pray that all creation, freed from slavery, may ever serve and praise God.

First Reading   Ezekiel 34:11-12.15-17

Though sometimes giving the impression of being physically present in Jerusalem, the prophet Ezekiel's mission was carried out among the exiles in Babylon in the early decades of the sixth century BC.

The image of a shepherd-king was common in the religious literature of the Middle East. Through Ezekiel, God rebukes and rejects the Jewish leaders for their negligent and selfish shepherding and asserts that he will assume the duties himself, protecting, feeding, healing and rescuing the people. He will also be their judge.

Psalm 22 (23)

The Lord is my shepherd;
there is nothing I shall want.

The first part of this psalm speaks of God fulfilling the duties of a shepherd for his flock, the Jewish people; in the second part, God's overall loving kindness is expressed in other ways.

Second Reading   1 Corinthians 15:20-26.28

In this extract from his first letter to the Corinthians, St Paul speaks of the triumph of Christ. Through his death and resurrection, he has won eternal life for all human beings. He has overcome all his enemies, the last of them being death itself. Then, finally, he will hand over all creation to the Father so that everything may be subject to him.

Gospel   Matthew 25:31-46

In his final report of Christ's public life and teaching before the Last Supper, Matthew describes the last judgment of all generations of the human race. We will be judged good or evil by our works of mercy (or lack of them) and those favourably judged by 'the King' will receive their inheritance in the kingdom of God. It is no surprise that Jesus judges using the criterion of our compassion for those in need, for that was the guiding principle of his own life on earth. In fact, the judge identifies himself with those in need, so our conduct in life (being with Christ, as he is present in the needy, or neglectful of him) determines our eternity also.

The Sunday Collects and Readings of Year B

Advent and Christmas, Year B

First Sunday of Advent • Year B

'Advent' means 'coming' and therefore, for us, it involves a time of 'waiting'.
But this should be understood as having a sense of 'desire' and 'expectancy'.

Collect

We pray that we may meet Jesus when he comes and that he will take us into the kingdom of God.

First Reading   Isaiah 63:16-17; 64:1.3-8

From the third part of the book of Isaiah. This final part of the prophecy dates from the return of the Jews from their exile in Babylon in the sixth century BC. On behalf of the people, the prophet pleads with God to come back and once again be their leader and Father. He deplores the sinful conduct of the people when God is not with them.

Psalm 79 (80)

God of hosts, bring us back;
let your face shine on us and we shall be saved.

The psalm is a plea for the restoration of the unity of Israel following conquest and ruin. The verses chosen for today are less specific and beseech God to protect and help his errant people.

Second Reading   1 Corinthians 1:3-9

From St Paul's first letter to the church at Corinth. The apostle praises and thanks God for his generosity in blessing the Christians in Corinth with so many graces. He adds that they are thus well prepared to wait for the coming of Christ. The reference here is, of course, to the second coming of our Saviour at the end of the world, an event that many Christians of the early Church expected to be imminent.

Gospel   Mark 13:33-37

Today we begin Year B, the 'Year of Mark'.

The passage chosen for today comes at the very end of Mark's account of Christ's public ministry, just before his passion and death. As in the second reading, the advice to be awake and prepared is in reference to the Lord's second coming (often termed the 'parousia'). The encouragement to 'stay awake' may be needed because the Lord's expected arrival has not occurred and the early fervour is cooling.

Second Sunday of Advent • Year B

Advent is a time of waiting, but our waiting should be a 'looking forward' with joy and hope. Today's liturgy is about the coming of Christ, the Messiah, but not specifically about his birth at Bethlehem.

Collect

May God help us to be eager to meet his Son and to have the faith we need in order to be in his company.

First Reading   Isaiah 40:1-5.9-11

From the section called Second Isaiah (or Deutero-Isaiah) and known as 'The Book of the Consolation of Israel' (see p.73). The context is the antici-pated release of the captive Israelites from exile in Babylon (a release which occurred in 538 BC).

God orders his prophet to proclaim the release and the journey home, all achieved through God's power and care for his chosen people. The Exodus is to be repeated and God is likened to a caring shepherd. (The 'voice' in verse 5 is God's but, in the Greek version, the meaning is changed from 'A voice cries, "Prepare in the wilderness..."' to 'A voice cries in the wilderness, "Prepare..."')

Psalm 84 (85)

Let us see, O Lord, your mercy
and give us your saving help.

The psalm is a prayer to God to bring exiles back to Israel, to live there in peace, justice and prosperity. The verses used lay stress on the latter theme, rather than the longing for deliverance. Christians interpret the psalm as messianic.

Second Reading   2 Peter 3:8-14

From the second letter of Peter. (Though most now consider the authorship very uncertain and perhaps by a disciple of Peter, the letter is 'canonical' i.e., rightly included in the Scriptures). The subject of this passage is the parousia. Some possible reasons for its delay are suggested and the people are warned to wait prepared and in readiness. Some details about the end of the world are mentioned. The theme of the reading is Christ's second coming.

Gospel   Mark 1:1-8

The opening lines of Mark's gospel (which has nothing about the infancy of Jesus). The evangelist quotes some words from Isaiah (today's first reading) but using the Greek text and so the 'voice' is identified as that of John the Baptist. We are then told some details about him and especially that, in his preaching, he was careful to speak of Jesus as 'more powerful' than he is, especially regarding his baptism which is 'with the Holy Spirit'. Nevertheless, John attracts many people and, since he preaches in the desert, that is the best place to find repentance and conversion.

Third Sunday of Advent • Year B

'Are you the one for whom we are waiting?' This question is still being asked today.

Collect

Looking forward to the feast of Christ's nativity, we ask God to enable us to obtain the salvation that Jesus brings and to celebrate that grace with true joy.

First Reading   Isaiah 61:1-2.10-11

From the prophecy of Isaiah, its third and final section (chapters 56-66). This section seems to be a mixture of authors and times, but today's passage (chapter 61) is similar to Second Isaiah and so it presumes that release from exile is imminent. The prophet rejoices in having received his mission from God. This is the passage which Jesus chose to read to the people in the synagogue in Nazareth and which he then applied to himself.

Psalm   Luke 1:46-50.53-54

My soul rejoices in my God.

These are selected verses from the Magnificat, the canticle of praise with which, according to Luke, Mary responded to her cousin's words of welcome to 'the mother of my Lord'. The canticle has some similarity to that of Hannah, the mother of Samuel (1 Samuel 2:1-10) but, in the Magnificat, Mary speaks in very personal terms of God's goodness to her as well as the divine option for the poor in general.

Second Reading   1 Thessalonians 5:16-24

From the first letter of St Paul to the Thessalonians. These are the closing words of the first extant letter of Paul. He sent several letters to the various churches which he had established in Greece (as here) and in Asia Minor. The words are of encouragement and advice and, among them, Paul mentions the awaited 'coming of our Lord Jesus Christ' (without further elaboration of its imminent happening).

Gospel   John 1:6-8.19-28

From the first chapter of St John's gospel. The evangelist speaks of John the Baptist, his mission and his witness about Jesus. As well as making it clear that he was not the expected messiah, the Christ, John the Baptist quotes Isaiah's words (last week's first reading) but in the sense that he, John (and not God), is the 'voice' in the desert. He alludes to 'the one who is coming after me' and who is more important than he is (in similar fashion to Mark's gospel, read last Sunday).

Fourth Sunday of Advent • Year B

With the feast of Christmas now only days away, today's Mass and especially the readings concentrate only on the first coming of the Lord.

Collect

This prayer, already well known to many of us, expresses our awareness of Christ's coming among us as man and asks God for the grace that, through his Son's passion and death, we may share in his resurrection.

First Reading   2 Samuel 7:1-5.8-12.14.16

From the Second Book of Samuel. This extract is built on a contrast. King David, though he wanted to, is not to build a house (a temple) for God; but God is to build a house (a dynasty) for David. The passage also speaks of God's special favours for David, which include the perpetuity of his line – the first in a series of prophecies about a messiah of David's line.

Psalm 88 (89)

I will sing forever of your love, O Lord.

The theme of today's first reading becomes even more explicit. The verses we use contain exchanges of loving fidelity between God and King David. God's covenant with David will last through the generations of his descendants.

Second Reading   **Romans 16:25-27**

In the final verses from his letter to the Romans, St Paul proclaims the Good News, now revealed, that God has sent Jesus Christ to be the crucial element in the divine plan for all human beings.

Gospel   **Luke 1:26-38**

The account of the incarnation of Jesus in the virginal womb of Mary. Luke's is the only gospel to narrate the story of the incarnation. His accounts of the conception and birth of Jesus and of John the Baptist form a parallel in his gospel. Yet there are great contrasts between the two: the place of the angels' announcements (in the temple in Jerusalem versus in a dwelling house in an obscure village in Galilee) and the parents (an elderly couple, the man being a venerable temple priest versus an insignificant young peasant virgin).

The Nativity of the Lord (Mass during the night): *see page 29*

The Nativity of the Lord (Mass at dawn): *see page 30*

The Nativity of the Lord (Mass during the day): *see page 31*

The Holy Family • Year B

The Holy Family is different from every other human family. Is it realistic to present it as the model for our families?

Collect

We ask God to help us to imitate the Holy Family and to practise their virtues in the lives of our own families.

Readings 1 & 2 and the Psalm for Year A (Ecclesiasticus 3:2-6.12-14, Psalm 127 (128), Colossians 3:12-21) may be read today. See p.32. Otherwise, the alternatives below are used.

First Reading   Genesis 15:1-6; 21:1-3

Abraham and Sarah have a son as promised by God who assures Abraham that his descendants will be innumerable.

Psalm 104 (105)

He, the Lord, is our God.
He remembers his covenant for ever.

Today's verses are the earliest of a long psalm which successively recounts the story of God's protection of his people from the time of Abraham to their arrival in the Promised Land.

Second Reading   Hebrews 11:8.11-12.17-19

The reading recalls the faith which Abraham and Sarah placed in God. Three examples of their faith are recalled, including that recounted in the first reading.

Gospel   Luke 2:22-40

Since Mark's Gospel lacks any information on Our Lord's childhood, Luke's account of the Presentation in the Temple is read. Mary and Joseph carefully observed all the requirements of the Jewish Law and made the offering that poor people made. We also read about Simeon and his words of prophecy to Mary; and we learn that Anna was present and subsequently told people about this child in terms of God's promise of a messiah. The passage ends with a few words on the childhood of Jesus.

Solemnity of Mary, the Holy Mother of God: *see page 33*

Second Sunday after the Nativity: *see page 34*

The Epiphany of the Lord: *see page 35*

The Baptism of the Lord • Year B

All four evangelists report this event, implying the importance of recording it as the start of Jesus' public ministry. What is the meaning of Jesus asking to be baptised by John?

Collect

At the baptism of Jesus, the Father declared him his beloved Son. We recall that, by baptism and the Holy Spirit, God has adopted us as his sons and daughters.

Readings 1 & 2 and the Psalm for Year A (Isaiah 42:1-4. 6-7, Psalm 28 (29), Acts 10:34-38) may be read today. See p.36. Otherwise, the alternatives below are used.

First Reading   Isaiah 55:1-11

The final chapter of Deutero-Isaiah is a fitting conclusion of the 'Book of the Consolation of Israel'. The return of the Jews from exile is foreseen as an era of God's favour for his covenanted people, a time of both spiritual and material prosperity.

Psalm   Isaiah 12:2-6

With joy you will draw water from the wells of salvation.

This 'psalm' is a hymn in First Isaiah. Although pre-exilic and therefore considerably earlier than the first reading, it is a fitting response to God's constant care for his people proclaimed there (as well having messianic relevance for Christians).

Second Reading   1 John 5:1-9

This extract from St John's first letter speaks of God's gifts to us of faith and love. The reasoning is rather complicated. If we love God, we will also love all God's creatures; loving God implies obeying his commandments; faith enables us to do this. The 'three witnesses' (water, blood and Spirit) are evidence of Christ's divine mission and also evidence of the new life of Christians acquired through the sacrificial death of Jesus (blood), our baptism (water) and the gift of the Spirit.

Gospel   Mark 1:7-11

St Mark's account of the baptism of Jesus by John the Baptist. Jesus shows humble solidarity with the people to whom he has been sent to bring salvation in God's kingdom. The Baptist declares the superiority of the baptism and mission of Jesus. The Holy Spirit comes down on Jesus and the Father proclaims him his beloved and trusted Son.

Lent and Easter, Year B

Ash Wednesday: *see page 37*

First Sunday of Lent • Year B

Collect

We pray that, by our Lenten activities, we may discover and gain the riches God has prepared for us.

First Reading   Genesis 9:8-15

In the book of Genesis, God speaks to Noah after the flood. The covenant which God makes with Noah includes the whole of creation, whereas the later covenants with Abraham and Moses are restricted to God's chosen people.

Psalm 24 (25)

Your ways, Lord, are faithfulness and love
for those who keep your covenant.

The Jews, returned from exile, look forward to a happy future and closeness with God. The verses used at this Mass thank God for the love and mercy he shows us and seek his guidance for the future.

Second Reading   1 Peter 3:18-22

The first letter of Peter has, as its main theme, fortitude in trial (perhaps written during a persecution) and with Jesus as the model for this.

The extract today, whose meaning is rather obscure, speaks of Christ's 'descent into hell' after his death (as we proclaim in the Creed). The author seems to say that the souls released from 'hell' by Christ had previously been drowned in the flood which, therefore, was a type or foretaste of baptism (whose efficacy comes through Christ, now risen and at God's right hand).

Gospel   Mark 1:12-15

Without details of the devil's temptations, Mark's account of Jesus in the desert is very brief. Nevertheless, note that it was God's Spirit that 'drove' Jesus into the desert, even though it was a place of wild beasts as well as protecting angels. (Is this being copied today with Christ's Church?) Mark then reports that Jesus went to Galilee and began to announce God's kingdom and the need to repent and believe.

Second Sunday of Lent • Year B

Collect

We pray to the Father that, having listened to his beloved Son, we may be enabled to witness the Father's glory.

First Reading   Genesis 22:1-2.9-13.15-18

God tests Abraham's faith to the utmost by ordering him to kill his only son Isaac as a sacrifice. When it is clear that Abraham will be obedient, an angel stops him and he offers a ram instead. God rewards Abraham's great faith by promising that his descendants will be innumerable, revered and successful over all their enemies. The story is the origin of the prescription that all first born have to be offered to God and then 'redeemed'. It is also used as an argument against any practice of child-sacrifice. ('Moriah' is traditionally believed to be the later site of the temple in Jerusalem, nowadays occupied by the Dome of the Rock.)

Psalm 115 (116)

I will walk in the presence of the Lord
in the land of the living.

This psalm of thanksgiving is appropriate for the first reading, particularly today's response which, in fact, occurs several times in the full version of the psalm.

Second Reading   Romans 8:31-34

This enthusiastic praise of God's love for us occurs at the end of chapter 8 of Paul's letter to the Romans. The mercy of the Father and Son are unlimited. That God did not even spare his own Son is a reminder of the first reading.

Gospel   Mark 9:2-10

The gospel on the 2nd Sunday of Lent is always the story of the transfiguration; today, it is from Mark's gospel, this being 'the Year of Mark'. Three apostles are present at the event at which Jesus is declared God's beloved Son. Moses and Elijah, representing the Law and prophets of the old covenant, are there as witnesses of God's approval of Jesus. The apostles are warned by Jesus to say nothing to anyone about what had happened; probably because Jesus did not want to be mistaken as a triumphant king come to overthrow the Roman army of occupation.

The transfiguration, occurring as it does while Jesus and the apostles are on their way south from Galilee to Judea where there will be hostility and indeed suffering and death for Jesus, is a reassurance that the journey is in accordance with God's will.

Third Sunday of Lent • Year B

We should keep in mind that Lent is not only a season for conversion and for getting ready for Easter, but also a time of preparation for baptism, either to be received or to be remembered with its commitment renewed.

Collect

As sinners, we ask God's mercy, acknowledging also his teaching that fasting, prayer and almsgiving are remedies for sin.

> *(The Readings for Year A on 3rd, 4th and 5th Sundays of Lent are appropriate for those preparing for baptism at the Easter Vigil. They should be used in parishes and communities in any year when there are to be such baptisms; they can in fact be used each year in any parish or community, if so desired. See pages 40-42.)*

First Reading   Exodus 20:1-17

The Ten Commandments, given by God to Moses, appear twice in the Pentateuch, once in the book of Exodus (as here) and once in the book of Deuteronomy (5:6-21). They include both instructions and prohibitions and form the core of the Mosaic Law (i.e., 'the law of Moses'). They are still binding on us, Christ having added 'the evangelical counsels' to perfect the Law. When St Paul rejects the Law, it is only to discard other rules added to the essentials and which some early Christians wished to continue to observe. (Christians differ in enumerating the ten commandments, some dividing into first and second what others consider only the first; the former then reckon as the tenth what the latter, including Catholics, divide into ninth and tenth.)

Psalm 18 (19)

You, Lord, have the message of eternal life.

The verses used today contain a reflection on God's precepts, praising their justice and reasonableness.

Second Reading   1 Corinthians 1:22-25

In the first chapter of the first letter to the church in Corinth, Paul compares the content of his teaching with what non-Christians demand. The latter regard Christian teaching as either objectionable or crazy, yet it is a sign of God's power and wisdom.

Gospel   John 2:13-25

All four gospels narrate this incident of Jesus driving the sellers and money changers out of the temple in Jerusalem, but John places it early in the public ministry while the synoptics narrate it as having occurred near the end. (Scripture commentators say that it is the event's meaning, rather than its timing, that is important). John adds the Jews' objections that followed Christ's actions and then their misunderstanding of Our Lord's use of the word 'temple'. Today's gospel passage ends with the remark that, while in Jerusalem for the Passover feast, Jesus attracted many people, but that he realised their fickle unreliability.

Fourth Sunday of Lent • Year B

Collect

We ask God to help us to prepare eagerly for the celebration of the Easter mysteries.

First Reading   2 Chronicles 36:14-16.19-23

This reading is the last part of the second book of Chronicles, written in the third century BC to give the history of Israel (partly repeating the books of Samuel and of Kings, partly giving some new details). This passage tells of the grievous sins and infidelity of the Jews, God's punishment in consigning them to exile in Babylon, and eventually his merciful release of the people and their return to their homeland.

Psalm 136 (137)

> *O let my tongue*
> *cleave to my mouth*
> *if I remember you not!*

This is the lament of the exiles in Babylon, Jerusalem having been captured and pillaged in 587 BC (see p.11).

Second Reading   Ephesians 2:4-10

The letter to the Ephesians may in fact be a general letter from Paul to all the Christian churches of Asia Minor and mainland Greece, written from prison in Rome towards the end of his life. This excerpt reminds us that God's plan of salvation for us is not merited but is sheer gift, a grace received through faith.

Gospel   John 3:14-21

St John's gospel recounts the meeting of Jesus with Nicodemus, a pharisee. After having told him that we must be reborn from above through water and the Spirit, Jesus (in today's excerpt) explains that God has sent 'the Son of Man' to be 'lifted up' so that, through our belief in him, we can be saved. There is an analogy between this reference to Christ on the cross and the bronze serpent which God told Moses to raise on a pole so that the Jews, while in the desert from Egypt, would not die even if they were bitten by serpents (Numbers 21:6-9). Jesus says that he was sent not to condemn people but to save them. He speaks of himself as the light and says that only sinners avoid the light and prefer the dark so as to conceal the evil they do. (The term 'Son of Man' which Jesus frequently calls himself is derived from its use in the Old Testament and especially the book of Daniel. Basically it merely means 'a man' but, in the context, it is used to denote someone special.)

Fifth Sunday of Lent • Year B

Collect

We ask God to give us the kind of love that enabled his Son to sacrifice his life for our sake.

First Reading   Jeremiah 31:31-34

The prophet Jeremiah was born around 646 BC and, when Jerusalem fell and many Jews were taken from Judea to exile in Babylon in 587, Jeremiah remained in Jerusalem but later had to flee to Egypt, where he died. Although a gentle person as well as God-fearing, his prophecies often spoke of disasters and of God's punishment for evil deeds. Today's excerpt, however, which comes from that part of Jeremiah's writing known as the Book of Consolation, is a beautiful passage in which the prophet speaks of God's forgiveness of the people and the institution of a new covenant with them.

Psalm 50 (51)

A pure heart create for me, O God.

Psalm 50 (51) is known as the *Miserere*, from the opening words 'Have mercy'. The psalm, and especially the verses today, ask God's mercy and forgiveness for our sins.

Second Reading   Hebrews 5:7-9

The letter to the Hebrews, whose author is unknown, was addressed to a group of Hebrew converts exiled from Jerusalem who were suffering persecution and tempted to revert to Judaism. The letter seeks to dissuade them. Today's short passage speaks of Christ as God's Son, humble, obedient to the Father, a compassionate Saviour.

Gospel   John 12:20-33

John's gospel today describes events in Jerusalem just before the Passover which coincides with the Paschal Mystery of Christ's passion, death and resurrection. The mention of the 'Greeks' (non-Jewish converts to Judaism or perhaps pagan visitors) is a reminder of the universality of God's plan of salvation and not necessarily that they heard the subsequent words of Jesus.

The remainder of the gospel passage is a passionate discourse of Jesus, summarising the profound meaning of his life. He first reflects on his coming death and then speaks of his anguish and yet of his obedience to the Father's will, publicly approved by 'a voice from heaven'. Jesus speaks of the combined glorification of both the Father and himself that will be achieved. This will come about not through a single event but by the entire life of Jesus, including his being 'lifted up' on the cross and at his resurrection/ascension. He will fulfil God's eternal plan: 'I shall draw all men to myself'.

Palm Sunday of the Passion of the Lord: *see page 43*

Thursday of the Lord's Supper: *see page 44*

The Celebration of the Passion of the Lord: *see page 45*

The Easter Vigil: *see page 46*

Easter Sunday: *see page 48*

Second Sunday of Easter • Year B

It is noteworthy that the Roman Missal (2011) gives an alternative designation for this Sunday: 'The Sunday of Divine Mercy'.

Collect

We seek a deeper faith and a better appreciation of God's generous gifts to us, namely, Christ our redeemer, the Holy Spirit who gives us new life, and baptism itself by which we have access to Jesus and the Spirit.

First Reading   Acts 4:32-35

Until Pentecost, the first readings on Sundays are from the Acts of the Apostles. In chapter 4, we have a second summary (the first is in chapter 2) of the activities of the first Christian community in Jerusalem. The apostles' witness to Christ's resurrection was accompanied by miracles. But Luke, the author of Acts, gives more space to the group's readiness to pool all they owned.

Psalm 117 (118)

Give thanks to the Lord for he is good,
for his love has no end. or *Alleluia, alleluia, alleluia!*

A hymn of thanksgiving, extolling God's love and care for his people.

Second Reading   1 John 5:1-6

The Sunday second readings until Pentecost are from the first letter of St John. It was written to the Christian communities in Asia Minor, some of whom were having problems with heretical tendencies. St John insists on lives of integrity, stressing faith in Jesus Christ and fraternal love. These two essentials are prominent in today's extract.

Gospel   John 20:19-31

In John's gospel, we read of two appearances of Jesus to the apostles in Jerusalem, the first on the first Easter Sunday and the second (when Thomas, absent earlier, was present) on the following Sunday. On the first occasion, Jesus confers the Holy Spirit on the apostles with the power of forgiving sin; on the second, Thomas humbly confesses his faith in the risen Lord. Jesus declares that the Gospel itself, which is the power of God, will be and is the adequate motive of our faith.

Note that, just as the apostles were slow to believe, merely on others' testimony, that the Lord had risen, Jesus can be hidden even in the Church today; it is our task to place him clearly at the heart of our communities.

Third Sunday of Easter • Year B

Collect

As we rejoice in our adoption as God's children, we look forward to even greater rejoicing at the resurrection of our bodies.

First Reading   Acts 3:13-15.17-19

After Pentecost, one day Peter and John had attracted a large crowd by curing a cripple of his lameness. Peter took the opportunity to instruct them and it is from his words that today's reading is taken. He shows the wrong that had been done to Jesus in demanding his execution but the people had not been aware of the evil they were doing. In fact, God had used their action in his plan for our salvation. However, they had to repent in order to have their sins 'wiped out'.

Psalm 4

Lift up the light of your face on us, O Lord.   or   *Alleluia!*

This psalm is really an evening prayer and intends to show our love of God and our trust in him.

Second Reading   1 John 2:1-5

St John tells us not to sin; but, if we do, Jesus died to remove our sins. And to know God, we have to keep the commandments; if we do that, we shall experience the perfect love of God for us.

Gospel   Luke 24:35-48

In Luke's gospel, we learn that the disciples who had met Jesus on the road to Emmaus had returned to Jerusalem and were telling their story to the community when Christ also joined them. Despite his greeting of 'Peace be with you', they were alarmed and afraid and thought he was a ghost. So to show that he has a body, he invites them to touch him and he eats some food. After that, he tells them that all that had happened - passion, resurrection, forgiveness of sins – was a fulfilment of what the Scriptures foretold.

Fourth Sunday of Easter • Year B

Although today we pray especially for those whom God calls to the ordained priesthood and to consecrated life, do not be misled: God calls all of us who are baptised to be active and effective witnesses of his Son.

Collect

Our Good Shepherd has gone to eternal life. We ask God that the sheep of the flock may follow him there.

First Reading   Acts 4:8-12

As a sequel to the cure of the cripple (last week's reading), Peter and John were arrested by the temple authorities and, next day, were put on trial before the Great Sanhedrin of Jerusalem, the supreme religious court (whose members were elders, scribes and former high priests). Peter takes the opportunity of witnessing that it was in the name of Jesus, sent by God to save us all from our sins, that he cured the cripple. (The court's verdict, not included in today's extract, was a strict warning not to preach about Jesus again.)

Psalm 117 (118)

*The stone which the builders rejected
has become the corner stone.*   or   *Alleluia!*

Originally for the Jewish feast of tabernacles, this psalm praises and thanks God for his love, care and protection.

Second Reading   1 John 3:1-2

Another reading from St John's first letter. Because God loves us, he has adopted us to be his children. So he must have even greater things awaiting us when we shall actually be able to see him.

Gospel   John 10:11-18

God already has declared himself the shepherd of his people and has promised to send a shepherd in the messianic age (Ezekiel 34:23-31). So here Jesus claims to be that shepherd- messiah. He is the good shepherd who knows, loves and tends his sheep and will even die for them. There will be other sheep so that there will be only one flock and Jesus the one shepherd.

Fifth Sunday of Easter • Year B

Collect

We ask God to bring the paschal mystery to fulfilment in us so that, after baptism, we may advance in goodness and reach eternal happiness.

First Reading   Acts 9:26-31

In this passage from the Acts of the Apostles, we hear of Saul/Paul's arrival in Jerusalem after his conversion. The disciples were at first very suspicious of him. Then his fearless preaching produced antagonism from the hellenists (Jews who had adopted Greek culture and customs); for his own safety, he was sent by sea to his home town of Tarsus. Thereafter the Christians in Palestine had a period of peace with increasing numbers and the joy of the Holy Spirit.

[In the letter to the Galatians, Paul tells us that, after his conversion and some time spent preaching in Damascus, he went to Arabia then back to Damascus; three years passed before his visit to Jerusalem (Galatians 1:17-18)].

Psalm 21 (22)

You, Lord, are my praise in the great assembly.   or   *Alleluia!*

This psalm, which begins with *My God, my God, why have you forsaken me?* and expresses the sufferings and the hope of a good man, ends with the verses of today's psalm. These speak of our veneration of God, caring and faithful.

Second Reading   1 John 3:18-24

St John urges that our love be sincere and therefore pleasing to God. And God will give us whatever we ask if we keep his commandments. These are to believe in his Son Jesus and to love one another. If we live thus and even if our conscience reproaches us, we can be reassured since God is a more understanding and lenient judge than we are.

Gospel   John 15:1-8

The prophets Isaiah and Jeremiah use the image of the vine (which fails to give the expected fruit) as an image of Israel (which has displeased God). St John tells us that, at the Last Supper, Jesus uses the vine image but in a different way. He is the 'true vine' and we are the branches. God tends the vine, removing branches that have no fruit and pruning those that have (a necessary task to keep the vine healthy and productive). Jesus continues to use and develop the image of the vine in this teaching discourse, whose crucial phrase is 'Cut off from me you can do nothing'.

Sixth Sunday of Easter • Year B

Collect

May our celebration and remembrance of Christ's saving death and resurrection bring us joy and always guide our lives in accordance with what is right.

First Reading   Acts 10:25-26.34-35.44-48

The Acts of the Apostles recounts the crucial development of Christianity, namely that God clearly shows that gentiles can receive the Holy Spirit and faith. As a result, Peter baptises the Roman centurion Cornelius, his relations and close friends in Caesarea. (This happened and, despite initial criticism in Jerusalem, became accepted practice. Similarly, despite doubts and disputes for a time, agreement was reached that gentiles who became Christians did not need to submit to the Mosaic Law, especially on circumcision.)

Psalm 97 (98)

> *The Lord has shown his salvation to the nations.*   or   *Alleluia!*

A song of praise to God who has revealed his salvation for all, both Jews and gentiles.

Second Reading   1 John 4:7-10

St John urges us to love one another since love is a gift of God who showed his love for us by sending his Son to save us from sin and give us life.

Gospel   John 15:9-17

Today's gospel continues from last week's and comes from Christ's discourse to the apostles at the Last Supper. Jesus asks them to love each other and, by keeping his commandments, to remain in his love. This, he promises, will bring them joy in its fullness. He calls them his friends, not servants, and declares that the greatest love we can show others is to die for them. He reminds them that he has chosen them and given them a mission that is to be effective.

The Ascension of the Lord: *see page 54*

Seventh Sunday of Easter • Year B

Collect

We believe that Jesus our Saviour is with the Father in glory and we pray that he may also and always be present with us here on earth.

First Reading   Acts 1:15-17.20-26

In Acts we are told that, after Jesus had returned to the Father, the Eleven met and prayed constantly with Mary, mother of Jesus, and several disciples, both men and women. Today's reading tells us of an important decision and its outcome that occurred at this time – the replacement of Judas by Matthias.

Psalm 102 (103)

The Lord has set his sway in heaven. or *Alleluia!*

Today's verses express our gratitude for God's love, shown by his forgiveness and faithfulness.

Second Reading   1 John 4:11-16

Today's excerpt from the first letter of John follows immediately after that of last week. We learn that, by loving each other, God lives in us. Through our sharing in the presence of the Holy Spirit, there is a mutual indwelling of God and ourselves. This depends on our faith in Jesus as the Son of God sent to save the world.

Gospel   John 17:11-19

This is Christ's prayer to the Father during the Last Supper. He prays for the apostles to remain faithful to their mission and be protected from the evil one. Jesus asks his Father to consecrate the apostles in truth as they preach in a hostile world.

Pentecost Sunday: *see page 57*

The Most Holy Trinity • Year B

*The Trinity is the most mysterious of all mysteries, totally beyond our compre-
hension. However, God has revealed some aspects of the mystery. We should
be anxious to know these aspects as well as venerating and adoring the one
God of three Persons, equal in eternity and majesty.*

Collect

As God revealed the mystery of the Trinity by sending into our world the
divine Word and the Holy Spirit, we pray that we may believe with faith that
God is one in nature but three distinct Persons, Father, Son and Spirit.

First Reading   Deuteronomy 4:32-34.39-40

In the book of Deuteronomy (the last of the Pentateuch), Moses is addressing
the people as they near the land God promised to give them after their escape
from slavery in Egypt. He speaks of God's majesty and power and, at the same
time, his choice of the Israelites for special protection and favour. Therefore,
that the people may prosper in the land given them by God, they are to faithfully obey his laws and commandments.

Psalm 32 (33)

Happy the people the Lord has chosen as his own.

The psalm extols God's faithfulness, justice and love. He is all-powerful, yet
cares for and protects those who place their trust in him.

Second Reading   Romans 8:14-17

In the letter to the Romans, chapter 8, Paul teaches that both the Holy Spirit
and our own spirit tell us that God has adopted us as his children and we can
call God 'Abba' (an Aramaic familiar form of 'Father'). So, as God's children,
we are his heirs, indeed co-heirs with Jesus, sharing his suffering on earth and
his glory hereafter. Note that the three Persons of the Trinity figure in this text.

Gospel   Matthew 28:16-20

St Matthew is sparse with his information on Christ's post-resurrection
appearances, which are mentioned only briefly. Today's gospel passage, the
conclusion of Matthew's gospel, describes Jesus taking leave of the Eleven.
He formally commits the apostles to continue his mission and promises that
he will be with them always. They are to baptise those to whom they preach,
and to do so in the name of Father, Son and Spirit.

The Most Holy Body and Blood of Christ • Year B

*Although Holy Thursday and the Mass of the Lord's Supper solemnly com-
memorate Christ's gift of the Eucharist, our awareness that the following
day is Good Friday overshadows our celebration that day of the Eucharist's
institution. So this feast was inaugurated in the thirteenth century, first
in Liége and then throughout the world. Pope Urban IV commissioned St
Thomas Aquinas to compose the texts for the feast; they include the hymns*
Lauda Sion *and* Pange Lingua *(the final two verses of which are sung at
Benediction:* Tantum ergo Sacramentum).

Collect

On this feast, the opening prayer is addressed to God the Son. We pray to
him that we may be so devoted to the sacred mystery of the Eucharist that we
may receive the graces won by him in his work of salvation.

First Reading   Exodus 24:3-8

In this extract from the book of Exodus, Moses supervises the rites that
enabled the Israelites, as they neared the Promised Land, to make a solemn
ratification of all the commands and instructions that they had received, through
Moses, from God. The Israelites promised to obey all the rules that God gave
them and Moses sprinkled on them the blood of bullocks which had been
sacrificed, thus declaring that their covenant with God had been solemnised.

Psalm 115 (116)

*The cup of salvation I will raise;
I will call on the Lord's name.*   or   *Alleluia!*

This is a psalm of thanksgiving to God for all his kindnesses. It is a psalm
still used in Jewish ritual and is also associated with Christian eucharistic liturgy.

Second Reading   Hebrews 9:11-15

In the letter to the Hebrews, the author draws comparisons between Jewish worship and that established by Jesus himself. The Christian liturgy is the
fulfilment of the Jewish and is superior in its high priest, in its sacrifice, in its
sanctuary and in its effects. The priest is Christ, the sacrifice is his blood, the
sanctuary is heaven itself, the effect is the forgiveness of sins and an eternal
inheritance. Christ is the mediator of the new and eternal covenant between
God and his people.

Gospel Mark 14:12-16.22-26

The passage is from Mark's account of the Last Supper. From the details of its preparation, it is clear that it takes place in the context of the Passover meal (although the ritual elements of that meal are not mentioned; there are also discrepancies between the synoptics and John's gospel which make it difficult to know the day of the week on which the Last Supper took place). The remark about new wine in God's kingdom is a reminder of the eschatological aspect of the Eucharist.

Gospel

Sundays 2-34 in Ordinary Time, Year B

Second Sunday in Ordinary Time • Year B

Collect

We ask God the all-powerful to give peace to the world.

First Reading   1 Samuel 3:3-10.19

From the first book of Samuel. In the eleventh century BC, a man named Elkanah had two wives, one with children but the other, Hannah, was barren. She prayed to God for a child and at last God granted her wish and she and Elkanah had a child whom they named Samuel. In gratitude, Hannah dedicated the child to God and, when the infant was weaned, she took him to the temple, then at Shiloh, and placed him in the care of Eli, the priest. Our reading begins at this point, with Samuel now a boy. God's call of Samuel is the consecration of the latter to be a prophet.

Psalm 39 (40)

Here I am, Lord! I come to do your will.

The first part of this psalm is a song of thanksgiving and dedication to do God's will and proclaim his goodness. It is from this part of the psalm that today's responsorial psalm is taken, since the rest of the psalm is a cry of distress and a plea for rescue.

Second Reading   1 Corinthians 6:13-15.17-20

From now until the 14th Sunday in Ordinary Time, the second reading will be from the two letters which St Paul wrote to the church at Corinth, a seaport in Greece. The Christians there were beset with disputes and also had to live in a city that had the reputation of being 'a centre of pleasure and vice'. Paul spent a year and a half preaching in Corinth (AD 51 to mid-52). The two letters date from the year 57, but there was a previous letter, now lost.

In today's reading, Paul warns against sins of fornication. Our bodies belong to God, they are temples of the Spirit and, together, make up the body of Christ. They are destined by God for eternal life.

Gospel   John 1:35-42

This is Year B, and the readings from Mark will begin next Sunday.

John's account of Jesus receiving baptism from John the Baptist is fuller than Mark's because it reports the calling by Jesus of one of the Baptist's disciples, Andrew and, on the following day, of Andrew's brother, Simon. 'The next day', John's gospel tells us, 'Jesus decided to leave for Galilee' (where we shall meet him in Mark's gospel next week).

Third Sunday in Ordinary Time • Year B

Collect

The opening prayer asks the Father to guide us so that all our activities may be done in the name of Jesus and be pleasing to God.

First Reading   Jonah 3:1-5.10

The book of Jonah, fifth century BC, although written as a narrative, is not history but a made-up story. Jonah is a self-important prophet who 'knows best'. He preaches repentance to Nineveh, sure that the people there will pay no heed. When they do repent, he is angry and humiliated. (In the gospels, Jesus uses the story to teach the need for conversion from sin. For this purpose, he uses the well-known illustration, without implying any opinion on its historicity.)

Psalm 24 (25)

Lord, make me know your ways.

The psalm is a plea to God by a distressed person in danger. However, the verses used today do not mention these circumstances but, remembering God's love and mercy, ask for his guidance.

Second Reading   1 Corinthians 7:29-31

Many of the early Christians thought it likely that the parousia (the end of the world and Christ's return as judge) was imminent. In this chapter, Paul is not formally teaching but merely giving his opinion and advice on some questions about which he has been consulted on marriage and virginity. Today's excerpt suggests that, if the parousia is near, it would be better to be as detached as possible from worldly commitments.

Gospel   Mark 1:14-20

We start our weekly readings from Mark's gospel. Today, Our Lord begins his public ministry with words which succinctly provide the core of his teaching. Then he chooses his first four apostles – simple fishermen on the Sea of Galilee (also called the Lake of Tiberias or of Gennesaret) whom he calls without more ado and who respond immediately. Simon and Andrew had originally been disciples of John the Baptist and Jesus had met them there at the Jordan (John 1:40-42) but now they had returned to Galilee and Jesus recruits them definitively. The sudden abandonment of their work by them (and by James and John) illustrates the renunciation involved in discipleship.

Fourth Sunday in Ordinary Time • Year B

Collect

We pray to be able to give God genuine honour and to have a sincere love for everyone.

First Reading   Deuteronomy 18:15-20

The last book of the Pentateuch is Deuteronomy, a large section of which is the 'Deuteronomic Code' of laws and custom which the Israelites were to observe on reaching the Promised Land. The first reading today is an excerpt from this section in which Moses announces that God agrees with the people that he will not deal with them directly but through a prophet, a second Moses. This promise is the reason for the Jews' expectation of a messiah-prophet, while Christians see the promise fulfilled in Jesus.

Psalm 94 (95)

O that today you would listen to his voice!
Harden not your hearts.

This psalm was in daily use by the Israelites. It is also the introduction each day to the prayers of the Divine Office ('Prayer of the Church' or 'Breviary'). The psalm calls on us to worship God faithfully and not to rebel against him (as the Israelites in the wilderness did, at the places given the names Meribah (= dispute) and Massah (= temptation).

Second Reading   1 Corinthians 7:32-35

Following immediately after last week's excerpt from 1st Corinthians, Paul recommends the unmarried state which, he says, allows a person to give 'undivided attention to the Lord' while marriage brings other duties and concerns. Paul is not laying down laws in this passage, but only offering his thoughts.

Gospel   Mark 1:21-28

Jesus teaches 'with authority' in the synagogue of Capernaum, on the north shore of the Sea of Galilee and the town that was his base in Galilee for his public ministry. To general bewilderment, he exorcises a man possessed by a devil. Similar exorcisms occur elsewhere in the gospels. Scholars dispute: are these cases merely psychic disorders unrecognised as such at that time and to which Jesus accommodated his words and actions and for which the sacred writers had only the language of that time? Or did the presence of the Son of God as our Saviour threaten the kingdom of Satan and cause an intense response? There is no certainty, case by case.

Fifth Sunday in Ordinary Time • Year B

Collect

The prayer asks for God's care and protection so that, in all matters, we may be kept safe.

First Reading   Job 7:1-4.6-7

The book of Job is a literary masterpiece in which Job (who has suffered various disasters) and his friends dialogue on the true meaning of divine justice. The friends do little to console him (hence 'Job's comforters'). A man named Job may have existed centuries before the book was written, but the unknown author of this book uses the old story merely as a framework for his composition (perhaps fifth century BC). In this reading, Job reflects on his misery, his pain and his sense of hopelessness.

Psalm 146 (147)

Praise the Lord who heals the broken-hearted.   or   *Alleluia!*

The psalm praises God, the creator, the liberator of Israel, all-wise, refuge of the poor. Instead of echoing the first reading's content, today the psalm is its antidote.

Second Reading   1 Corinthians 9:16-19.22-23

St Paul, continuing his first letter to the Christians in Corinth, rejoices in the work God has given him, adding that his only reward is the satisfaction of sharing the Good News. His commitment to preaching the gospel is absolute and unconditional.

Gospel   Mark 1:29-39

The passage from Mark gives us glimpses of the activities of Jesus – healing the sick and the possessed in Capernaum, seeking solitude for prayer before dawn, going to many places all over Galilee, preaching and healing.

The so-called 'messianic secret', which is frequently mentioned in Mark, is evident for the first time. Jesus forbids the disciples to speak of him and especially of his cures because the common notion of the messiah as a leader to rid the country of the Romans and restore independence was in complete contrast with the purpose of his mission.

Sixth Sunday in Ordinary Time • Year B

Collect

We ask God to make our hearts fit places for him to dwell in.

First Reading   Leviticus 13:1-2.44-46

Leviticus is the third book of the Pentateuch and is almost entirely about laws which God imposed on the Jews. Chapter 13 is on leprosy (a term which included various skin diseases). Chapter 14 is on the ritual purification of leprosy, since the disease brought ritual uncleanness. Not only was genuine leprosy incurable, but the consequences of exclusion etc. for the victims were very severe.

Psalm 31 (32)

You are my refuge, O Lord;
you fill me with the joy of salvation.

The sinner confesses his sin to God who mercifully forgives him, to the sinner's joy.

Second Reading   1 Corinthians 10:31-11:1

St Paul encourages the Corinthians to imitate him (as he imitates Christ) in always acting for the benefit of others and not of themselves. Thus whatever they do should be done to give glory to God.

Gospel   Mark 1:40-45

Last week's gospel told of Christ's journey 'all through Galilee'. Today we read of the only cure specifically mentioned on that journey – the healing of a leper. Note that, according to the account, there were two infringements of the law: first, the leper approached Jesus and, second, Jesus touched him. There is also a further mention of the 'messianic secret'.

Seventh Sunday in Ordinary Time • Year B

Collect

A straightforward prayer in which we ask God that all that we say and do may be pleasing to him.

First Reading   Isaiah 43:18-19.21-22.24-25

From chapter 40 to chapter 55, the prophecy of Isaiah is normally called

Second Isaiah or Deutero-Isaiah. The earlier chapters belong to the eighth century BC and are pre-exile; these are from two centuries later, towards the end of the Jews' exile in Babylon and when they were anticipating a return home.

Today's reading is from chapter 43. God declares a good future for his people and pardon, even if undeserved, for their sins.

Psalm 40 (41)

Heal my soul for I have sinned against you.

The psalm declares God's protection from both extraneous and personal dangers. The declaration then becomes a plea for God's help, as well as for his pardon from sin.

Second Reading   2 Corinthians 1:18-22

Again Paul writes to the church at Corinth but, from today, it is the second letter. After the first letter was sent, serious trouble broke out in the church at Corinth and Paul made a brief visit to the city and then sent this 'second letter', so-called because Paul sent three letters to Corinth, but the first is not preserved. In today's passage, Paul states that his teaching has always been clear and neither confused nor confusing. The assertive tone is probably the result of the recent problems at Corinth.

Gospel   Mark 2:1-12

The fame and popularity of Jesus are evident on his return to his base at Capernaum, after his journey around Galilee (noted in the gospel excerpt two weeks ago). Jesus was preaching and healing (from sin as well as physical infirmities). Some scribes were present – men with great authority in Scripture interpretation and legal decisions, and with the right of Sanhedrin membership. Jesus and his followers had not spent similar years of study, hence the usual antagonism of the scribes who saw them as unqualified and therefore usurpers of their authority.

Eighth Sunday in Ordinary Time • Year B

Collect

A prayer for God's peace throughout the world and, in particular, that the Church may enjoy that gift.

First Reading   Hosea 2:16-17.21-22

Hosea is one of the twelve 'minor' (i.e., shorter) prophets. He lived in the northern kingdom of Israel in the eighth century BC, a time of turbulence there, of violence and disaster. Hosea's own life was also saddened by the infidelity of his wife. Hosea is the first author in Scripture to describe God's relationship with his chosen people in marital terms. This became common in the Old Testament and continues in the New, above all the relation of Christ and the Church. In today's reading, God determines to attract and treat Israel with great love. (The reference to the wilderness is because, on emerging from slavery into the desert, the people had shown total fidelity to God.)

Psalm 102 (103)

The Lord is compassion and love.

The psalm extols God's love for his people, but especially in the context of his readiness to forgive our sins.

Second Reading   2 Corinthians 3:1-6

In today's extract from 2nd Corinthians, Paul declares that the proof that his work is God's work comes from the evidence of the Spirit living in the hearts of his converts. The new covenant with God, preached by Paul, comes from the life-giving Spirit.

Gospel   Mark 2:18-22

In today's passage, the great difference between John the Baptist and Jesus in their preaching and messages becomes evident; the former is a message of fear and severe judgment, the latter of love and freedom. This is clear not only from the people's enquiry but also from the examples of the new patch and the new wine.

Ninth Sunday in Ordinary Time • Year B

Collect

We ask God, in his providence, to grant us what will be for our benefit and to keep from us whatever may harm us.

First Reading   Deuteronomy 5:12-15

Deuteronomy is the final book of the Pentateuch, the collective name given to the first five books of the Bible. Today's reading is an excerpt from Moses' teaching to the Jews on the Ten Commandments, before they entered the Promised Land; here, he is giving God's instruction on the third commandment.

Psalm 80 (81)

Ring out your joy to God our strength.

A suitable psalm with which to respond to the first reading. The feast referred to in the first verse is that of Tabernacles, which commemorated the Jews' period in the desert and the Law given by God on Mount Sinai; it was the greatest feast of the year. The third verse is a reference to the forced labour imposed on the Jews while in Egypt, while the final verse is a command to worship the one God and avoid idolatry.

Second Reading   2 Corinthians 4:6-11

In this passage from 2nd Corinthians, Paul speaks of the Good News of Christ, the Lord, the image of God, who, by his death and resurrection, is our Saviour and now lives in glory. But since Paul is only the instrument whereby the message is delivered, he has to endure constant trials and sufferings (as Jesus also did).

Gospel   Mark 2:23-3:6

Two other events in the life of Jesus are reported, both rousing the ire of the religious authorities – picking ears of corn on the sabbath and curing a withered hand also on the sabbath. The provocation is increased since Jesus speaks of himself as Son of Man and performs miracles. And his point is that laws (such as the strict interpretation of the sabbath) can wrongly ignore the needs and wellbeing of people.

Tenth Sunday in Ordinary Time • Year B

Collect

We pray that God, the source of all that is good, may guide us to discern and do what is right.

First Reading   Genesis 3:9-15

From the third chapter of the book of Genesis (first book of the Pentateuch and also of the Bible), God speaks to Adam and Eve, guilty of sin, and curses the being who induced them to sin – the devil, the enemy of God and man (and here described as a serpent). The final verse of the excerpt (verse 15) is called the 'proto-evangelium' (i.e., the earliest hint of God's plan of salvation) since it sees continuing conflict between the descendants of the devil and of the woman and the victory of the latter.

[*It will crush your head:* in Greek the pronoun is masculine hence understood as the messiah; in Latin the pronoun is feminine and therefore understood as Mary since she and her messiah-son are so united. In English . . .?!]

Psalm 129 (130)

With the Lord there is mercy
and fullness of redemption.

We use the whole of this psalm (the *De profundis*), familiar as a prayer for the dead. The psalm asks for God's forgiveness and, even more, declares our hope and trust in him.

Second Reading   2 Corinthians 4:13-5:1

Paul asserts his total faith that the God who raised Jesus from the dead will, after this life and its sufferings and troubles, do the same for us. Instead of our earthly tent, we shall dwell for ever in the house built for us by God.

Gospel   Mark 3:20-35

In today's passage from Mark's gospel, two serious matters are raised.

First, the relationship which Jesus had with his mother and relatives. Contact during his public ministry seems to have been infrequent and, for Jesus, his family had become 'anyone who does the will of God' (and whom God therefore adopts).

Second, the accusation that it is through Beelzebul (the Canaanite god 'Baal', literally 'Baal the Prince') that Jesus casts out devils. Jesus ridicules this but then condemns his accusers for an unforgivable sin since their denial of the Spirit's evident activity shows they have closed themselves to God's desire to give them saving grace.

Eleventh Sunday in Ordinary Time • Year B

Collect

Admitting our inability to do anything good without God's help, we ask for the grace to be obedient in both intention and deed.

First Reading   Ezekiel 17:22-24

The prophet Ezekiel lived during the years of the Jews' exile in Babylon and was active in the early decades of the sixth century BC, possibly for some of the time in Jerusalem before being later with the exiles. The excerpt is a prophecy of God's future restoration of the Jews to their homeland and to prosperity. It is seen as a prophecy of a messianic age.

Psalm 91 (92)

It is good to give you thanks, O Lord.

A psalm which rejoices in God's love for us and his truth and especially his care of the virtuous.

Second Reading   2 Corinthians 5:6-10

Writing in the second letter to the Corinthians, Paul anticipates the joy of being with Christ after he dies. Both now on earth and then, he wants to be pleasing to the Lord, aware that we shall be judged on our actions here on earth.

Gospel   Mark 4:26-34

Jesus describes God's kingdom on earth by using two parables which show that the kingdom will increase and develop, generally unnoticed and in virtue of its own intrinsic power. The final two sentences of today's gospel are puzzling. Do they mean that Jesus wanted only his close followers to understand fully? Is this another example of the 'messianic secret'?

Twelfth Sunday in Ordinary Time • Year B

Collect

Confident of God's continuing guidance, we pray that we may always live faithful to him.

First Reading   Job 38:1.8-11

From the book of Job, the great literary masterpiece of the Old Testament. The subject is God's justice in a world of much suffering: how can the two be reconciled? In today's very brief passage, we hear part of one of the speeches God makes. He declares his power and control over the mighty oceans.

Psalm 106 (107)

> *O give thanks to the Lord,*
> *for his love endures for ever.* or *Alleluia!*

The whole psalm is a hymn of thanksgiving to God for various mercies. Appropriately today we use the verses which give thanks for God's care of those who sail the seas.

Second Reading   2 Corinthians 5:14-17

Paul cannot contain his love for Christ when he thinks that Jesus died and rose to life – and that was done for us, so that we would be able to live a new life in Christ and for Christ.

Gospel   Mark 4:35-41

Jesus calms a storm which threatens the flotilla of ships carrying him and his disciples across the Sea of Galilee (Lake of Tiberias/Lake of Gennesaret). He chides his disciples for their lack of faith. They are amazed at his command of the storm. (Note the neat inter-connection of today's first reading, psalm and gospel.)

Thirteenth Sunday in Ordinary Time
• Year B

Collect

We pray that God, our Father by adoption, may keep us from the darkness of error and ensure that we always walk in the light of truth.

First Reading   Wisdom 1:13-15; 2:23-24

The book of Wisdom, though claiming Solomon as its author, is, from internal evidence, a composition of the middle of the first century BC by a Jew in Alexandria, writing to urge his fellow-Jews not to be influenced by the hellenist (i.e., Greek) culture of the city. In today's passage, the author declares that God neither wants nor decrees our death, either spiritual or physical; the devil and sin are responsible for death in both its forms. This teaching is a great advance on earlier Jewish vagueness about sheol (the underworld/hell).

Psalm 29 (30)

I will praise you, Lord,
you have rescued me.

This is a psalm which praises and thanks God for rescuing a person from imminent and serious danger.

Second Reading   2 Corinthians 8:7.9.13-15

Paul appeals to the Christians in Corinth to be generous in their material help to those in need and, specifically, to the church in Jerusalem. He is not asking the Corinthians to impoverish themselves but that they should remember the example of Jesus himself, who from his wealth became poor for our sake.

Gospel   Mark 5:21-43

Jesus heals two people. The circumstances are different. One concerns a child and from a prominent family; the miracle is requested and performed openly (though Jesus asks for the 'messianic secrecy'). The other cure is for a nameless, fearful and lonely women (a haemorrhage was regarded as making a person ritually unclean) and is done quietly and without fuss. But both events show the power and the love that Jesus possesses.

Fourteenth Sunday in Ordinary Time
• Year B

Collect

Recognising that our fallen world was raised up through Christ's humble acceptance of suffering, we pray that we may experience the lasting joy that our rescue from sin brings us.

First Reading   Ezekiel 2:2-5

Three weeks ago, the first reading was from Ezekiel, chapter 17; today it is again from Ezekiel, but chapter 2. The prophet is ordered by God to go and preach to the rebellious people of Israel. Note that Ezekiel is called 'son of man', a title which, first, the prophet Daniel and, then, Jesus later adopted for themselves. In itself, it simply means a male person but in both contexts (Ezekiel and Jesus) it takes on the sense of someone exceptional.

Psalm 122 (123)

Our eyes are on the Lord
till he show us his mercy.

The troubled Israelites plead for God's protection. The context may be the people's return from exile, fearful of the hostility of surrounding pagans.

Second Reading   2 Corinthians 12:7-10

The final excerpt from 2nd Corinthians, and from near the conclusion of Paul's letter. He speaks of 'a thorn in the flesh' for which he has prayed in vain to have removed. God has told him that he wants him to remain weak and humble since God's power 'is at its best in weakness'. The nature of the 'thorn' is unknown to us: a debilitating illness? the hostility of many Jews?

Gospel   Mark 6:1-6

Jesus visits Nazareth, his home town, and teaches in the synagogue on the sabbath. The reception was hostile. Nor could he perform any miracles since the people lacked faith.

[Note 'brothers and sisters', clearly not siblings but members of the extended family.]

Fifteenth Sunday in Ordinary Time • Year B

Collect

The light God gives maintains us in the truth or restores us to it; so we pray that, by God's help, all Christians may remain faithful to Christ and his teaching.

First Reading   Amos 7:12-15

Amos was a shepherd from Judah, called to preach in God's name, to a prosperous Israel where religion was largely superficial and the rich exploited the poor. His message was unwelcome, as Amaziah (a priest of Israel) told Amos, who replied that he was a reluctant prophet merely obeying God.

Psalm 84 (85)

Let us see, O Lord, your mercy and give us your saving help.

In this psalm, the Jews, returned from exile, are assured of God's gifts, and especially his peace, in a future messianic age.

Second Reading   Ephesians 1:3-14

For seven Sundays, the second reading will be from St Paul's letter to the Christians of Ephesus (a town near the west coast of Asia Minor). It is perhaps likely, however, that this letter was written not for any one local church but for them all. It responds to some problems and dangers that had arisen among Christians and develops theological themes already treated in the letters to the Romans and Corinthians. Even Paul's authorship is a matter of dispute among scholars; if he wrote the letter, he did so from prison, probably in Rome.

The letter opens with the passage chosen for today's second reading. It is an inspired and inspiring outline of God's eternal plan of salvation for the human race. Paul describes a number of gifts that God confers on his people through Christ the Saviour, gifts that begin to be received on earth and will be fully and perfectly enjoyed in eternal life. The idea pervading the letter is that creation was cut off from the Creator by sin but has been restored by Christ reuniting all its parts into an organism with himself as the head.

Gospel   Mark 6:7-13

Jesus initiates the Twelve into sharing his ministry of preaching and healing, a task which they begin successfully. His instructions to them require that they should live in poverty, dependent on the support of those to whom they ministered. [The other two synoptics recount the same details except that, while Mark allows the Twelve to carry staffs, Matthew and Luke forbid even that!]

Sixteenth Sunday in Ordinary Time • Year B

Collect

We ask God to be generous with his gifts and graces and pray that, with faith, hope and love, we may be more ready to obey him.

First Reading   Jeremiah 23:1-6

Jeremiah prophesied in the last decades of the seventh and the early decades of the sixth centuries BC, a very troubled period in Judah, including the siege and destruction of Jerusalem and its temple and the deportation of many citizens to Babylon. In today's passage God condemns the useless shepherds (rulers) and says that he will himself care for the people and ensure that there are good shepherds to look after them. The passage concludes with the messianic prophecy of a wise and good king for God's chosen people.

Psalm 22 (23)

The Lord is my shepherd;
there is nothing I shall want.

Appropriately, this well-known psalm is used today and in its entirety. God's care for his people is illustrated with two images: the good shepherd and the host at a banquet. The psalm is explicitly messianic.

Second Reading   Ephesians 2:13-18

Paul continues last week's teaching. Christ's death on the cross unites Jews and gentiles, reconciling both with the Father and enabling gentiles to share the Jews' privileged status with God. Hostility between the two is ended by Christ's death so that there is now 'one single New Man' and 'a single Body', the mystical body of Christ (the Church) in which Jesus is the Head and we are the members, each with its own function. And through Christ and in the Spirit, all of us have access to the Father.

Gospel   Mark 6:30-34

The Twelve return from their first missionary efforts and Jesus decides to take them away for rest and recuperation. But his plans are thwarted.

Seventeenth Sunday in Ordinary Time • Year B

Collect

We seek God's protection and his guidance to use wisely the things of this world as helps that will enable us to cling to the things that last.

First Reading   2 Kings 4:42-44

The two books of the Kings trace the history of the Jews from the time of Solomon (tenth century BC) until the destruction of Jerusalem and the deportation in 587 BC. After Solomon, the country split into the southern and northern kingdoms, the former being the kingdom of Judah (which included the city of Jerusalem) and the latter the kingdom of Israel (comprised of the other tribes). There was constant hostility and frequent warfare between the two.

Today's excerpt (ninth century BC) tells of Elisha, the successor of Elijah, and of a miracle of the multiplication of loaves for the feeding of a crowd.

Psalm 144 (145)

You open wide your hand, O Lord,
and grant our desires.

This psalm praises God and gives thanks for his generosity, making special mention of the food that he unfailingly provides.

Second Reading
Ephesians 4:1-6

Paul appeals to his readers to live in harmony with one another and to treat one another with unfailing kindness. This is not a mere hope but is based on the oneness of God and the unity of faith into which we are all baptised.

Gospel
John 6:1-15

Mark's gospel is the shortest of the three synoptics, too short to cover all the thirty-four Sundays of Ordinary Time. So for five Sundays (17th to 21st) a 'patch' is inserted, chapter 6 of John's gospel. This chapter possesses a coherence and unity that will be clear as we proceed. Today's passage opens the chapter by recounting the feeding by Jesus of five thousand who had followed him, impressed by his power of healing. The event and particularly the way in which the evangelist tells the story keep us mindful of our celebration of the Eucharist.

Eighteenth Sunday in Ordinary Time • Year B

Collect

With loving trust we ask God to repair what we have damaged of his creation and to save it from further harm.

First Reading
Exodus 16:2-4.12-15

The book of Exodus, the second book of the Pentateuch, gives an account of the Jews' forty years in the desert, journeying from slavery in Egypt to the Promised Land. In the wilderness of Sin in the Sinai Peninsula, they complain of lack of food; as a result God provides them with daily meat and bread (quails and manna).

Psalm 77 (78)

The Lord gave them bread from heaven.

This psalm is a teaching on the history of Israel and on the Israelites' duty to tell that story of God's care to each generation. The verses chosen recall today's first reading.

Second Reading   Ephesians 4:17.20-24

In this extract from the letter to the Ephesians, Paul urges the Christians to seek the grace of conversion to a holy manner of life.

Gospel   John 6:24-35

After the miracle of the loaves (which was last Sunday's gospel), many of those who had been fed there searched for Jesus and found him back in Capernaum. He tells them that their motive for seeking him is wrong. They should want the truly important nourishment that he, the Son of Man sealed at his baptism with God's Holy Spirit, can give them. The dialogue continues and can be expressed thus: 'So what does God want us to do?' 'You have to believe in him whom God has sent, namely, me.' 'We must have a sign to prove that we have to believe in you.' 'Although God sent bread, manna, in the desert, that was only a foretaste of God's true bread.' 'That is the bread we want.' 'I am the bread of life. If you believe in me, you will never lack anything.' (The inference, from John's view of Christ, is that Jesus is the personified Wisdom of God who reveals God's secret plans to us. To come to Jesus and believe in him is to learn to live like him.)

Nineteenth Sunday in Ordinary Time • Year B

Collect

Since the Holy Spirit assures us that we are adopted children of God, we pray that we may learn how to live out that privilege and reach our inheritance of eternal life.

First Reading   1 Kings 19:4-8

An incident in the life of the prophet Elijah (ninth century BC). He is fleeing for his life from King Ahab and Queen Jezebel. Near death from starvation, he is given food and water by an angel from God. He finally reaches Mount Horeb (an alternative name for Mount Sinai) where God had given the covenant to Moses. Elijah sees his work as a resumption of the work of Moses, keeping the people faithful to the covenant.

Psalm 33 (34)

Taste and see that the Lord is good.

The psalm praises and glorifies God for his unfailing help to those in need. Sometimes, an angel is sent as God's messenger of mercy (as in today's first reading).

Second Reading   Ephesians 4:30-5:2

The Holy Spirit keeps the Body of Christ united, so Paul urges us not to make the Spirit sad by disruptive behaviour. Indeed, as adopted children of God, we should imitate Jesus who sacrificed his life for love of us.

Gospel   John 6:41-51

The claim that Jesus has made (last week's passage) that he is the bread of life sent by God upsets his listeners. But Jesus only insists more strongly. To reach eternal life, he says, we must believe the teaching of God and, since only he, Jesus, has seen God, we must learn from him. Jesus repeats that he is the living bread from heaven and only by eating it will we reach eternal life. Today's passage ends with an astonishing declaration: the 'bread' of which Jesus is speaking is not only the nourishing teaching of God communicated to us by God's Word, but also his own flesh.

Twentieth Sunday in Ordinary Time • Year B

Collect

We ask God, by his own love, to bring us to love him more than everything else so that we may reach the inheritance with him that he has promised.

First Reading   Proverbs 9:1-6

The book of Proverbs is a collection from the 10th to the 5th centuries BC. This reading is from the section (probably fifth century) in which a father is instructing his son on wisdom. He describes wisdom as a hostess who will teach her art to those who accept the invitation to go to her house. ['Seven columns' in wisdom's house are merely because seven was regarded as the number of perfection.]

Psalm 33 (34)

Taste and see that the Lord is good.

A psalm praising God's wisdom and urging us to seek that same gift from God.

Second Reading   Ephesians 5:15-20

Paul encourages Christians to live good lives and to behave as God requires. We sing psalms and hymns when together and our praying should continue in our hearts even when we are alone. Thus we shall constantly show our gratitude to God our Father.

Gospel   John 6:51-58

The gospel passage today begins by repeating the final words of last week's excerpt: 'The living bread that I shall give is my own flesh'. Many there express their consternation at this claim, but Jesus simply emphasises it and does so several times: 'Anyone who eats my flesh and drinks my blood has eternal life . . .'.

Twenty-First Sunday in Ordinary Time
• Year B

Collect

We ask God to make us so obedient to him and so full of hope that, in this changing world, we may be intent on reaching the place of true happiness.

First Reading   Joshua 24:1-2.15-18

The book of Joshua describes the conquest of the Promised Land, its distribution among the twelve tribes, and Joshua's final address to all the Jews, an extract from which provides today's reading. Joshua challenges the people regarding their fidelity to the Lord, the one true God. The response is unanimous: 'The Lord alone will we serve'. He was, is and will be their God.

Psalm 33 (34)

Taste and see that the Lord is good.

This is the same psalm as was used for the previous two weeks but, apart from the opening verse, the other verses are from different parts of the psalm. The emphasis today is on God, the refuge of those in distress and the protector of the innocent victims of evil people.

Second Reading   Ephesians 5:21-32

This is the final extract from Paul's letter to the Ephesians. He draws a parallel between a human marriage and the union of Christ with the Church. Thus he sees the two unions as shedding light on each other. First, a husband loves his wife; so Christ loves the Church (and gives up his life for her). Second, Christ is the head of the Church and the Church submits to him; so likewise with husband and wife. Third, the Church is one with Christ as his body; so a husband leaves his parental home to be one with his wife, treating her just as if they were physically one. The passage makes use of the culture and customs of the time, not only in the husband being the head of his wife and she submitting to him, but also in the parallel attempted between baptism and the Middle Eastern custom of the bride's ritual bath before the wedding. These elements in the passage can cause misunderstanding or offence nowadays. Finally, in the penultimate sentence, Paul quotes the book of Genesis (2:24), adding that the text is a 'mystery' in the sense that it is a hidden prophecy, now revealed, of the marriage between Christ and the Church (as, in the Old Testament, Israel was sometimes called the bride or wife of God).

Gospel   John 6:60-69

The final excerpt from John, chapter six. Many disciples walk away from Jesus. He realises that this was likely because it is only through the Holy Spirit that understanding, belief and life can come. Without the Spirit's help (i.e., with only the flesh to assist), these would not be present. When Jesus asks the Twelve, Peter responds very positively: 'You are the messiah, your words bring eternal life, and we (note the plural pronoun) believe'.

Twenty-Second Sunday in Ordinary Time • Year B

Collect

We ask God, from whom we receive everything good, to help us to love him more, to increase his gifts in us and to protect them with his care.

First Reading   Deuteronomy 4:1-2.6-8

The book of Deuteronomy, in addition to a codification of religious and civil laws for the Jews, has several long discourses of Moses as the people prepared to cross the Jordan into the Promised Land. In today's reading, Moses expresses praise and thanks to God for all of God's commands and instructions and enjoins the people to observe them faithfully.

Psalm 14 (15)

The just will live in the presence of the Lord.

To the question, 'Who can be allowed to be in the presence of God?', this short psalm responds by offering a summary of good moral conduct.

Second Reading   James 1:17-18.21-22.27

For five Sundays, we have excerpts from the letter of James.

Its author is thought, by most, not to be either of the apostles of this name, but 'James, brother of the Lord', prominent in the early Christian community in Jerusalem and put to death about 62 AD. This first excerpt praises God for making us his children and urges us to be obedient to all that God tells us. In particular, we must help those in need and avoid the example of unbecoming conduct.

Gospel   Mark 7:1-8.14-15.21-23

After the Johannine 'patch', we resume Mark's gospel. Today's passage tells us of two encounters which Jesus had. The first is with some religious leaders who criticised his disciples for not observing various practices added to the laws that Moses received from God. Jesus replies by accusing them of hypocrisy, quoting from Isaiah in his rejection of their criticisms. Second, to the crowd in general, he says that what we eat does not make us unclean, but rather the evil deeds that we do.

Twenty-Third Sunday in Ordinary Time
• Year B

Collect

We ask God to grant us, his adopted family, that, believing in Christ, we may be truly free and reach our promised inheritance.

First Reading   Isaiah 35:4-7

In this poem from the prophecy of Isaiah, there is a sense of hope that God is about to renew the people and to restore their land. The passage can be seen as looking forward to the return from exile or, more distantly, to the expectation of a messiah.

Psalm 145 (146)

My soul, give praise to the Lord.   or   *Alleluia!*

This psalm is a morning prayer for Jews. It is a hymn of praise to God who is faithful in his help for those in need.

Second Reading   James 2:1-5

The letter of James, addressed to Jewish Christians, urges his readers not to treat the wealthy with a consideration denied to the poor. The passage ends by asserting that God has a special preference for the poor; this reminds us that, in his public ministry, Jesus showed a clear love and care for those who were poor and unimportant in the eyes of the powerful.

Gospel   Mark 7:31-37

Mark relates that Jesus had been in the district of Tyre. This is gentile territory and denotes that Jesus has come to save gentiles as well as Jews (although the latter have priority at the start). Back in Jewish territory, he cures a deaf-mute and, despite the orders of Jesus, the cure is made widely known.

[The actions and word (finger and spittle, the Aramaic 'ephphatha') used by Jesus are part of the rite of the sacrament of baptism, during which our ears are symbolically opened to hear God's word and our tongue loosened to spread it.]

Twenty-Fourth Sunday in Ordinary Time
• Year B

Collect

We ask God, our creator and ruler, to help us experience his mercy and willingly serve him.

First Reading   Isaiah 50:5-9

As last Sunday, this reading is also from Isaiah but from the later part, known as Second Isaiah (or Deutero-Isaiah) which belongs not to the eighth but to the sixth century BC, with the Jews in exile but with grounded hope of returning home soon. In this part, there occur the four 'songs of the servant of the Lord', today's reading being the third. The 'song' is of a perfect disciple of God who proclaims the true faith and suffers in atonement of others' sins, but is exalted at last by God. Christians understand the songs as messianic prophecy.

Psalm 114 (116)

I will walk in the presence of the Lord
in the land of the living.   or   *Alleluia!*

In this psalm, no.114 of the Greek text and the first half of no.116 in the Hebrew text, the psalmist gives thanks to God for his protection from danger and rescue from death. It is an appropriate response to the first reading of today.

Second Reading   James 2:14-18

The letter of James insists that, for salvation, we must have good works to show as well as faith. St Paul stresses the necessity of faith (for the radical sinfulness of our unredeemed condition prevents self-made sanctity), but he also admits that we must show our faith by good works; in this way, we obey the law of Christ, the commandment to love God and our neighbour. The two teachings are not irreconcilable, but the emphasis on faith and/or good works differs.

Gospel   Mark 8:27-35

Peter's profession of faith in Jesus as the Christ (and messiah) is also told in Matthew (where the profession is a little more detailed) and Luke. It is followed by Jesus foretelling his passion, death and resurrection. Peter remonstrates but is rebuked by Jesus in very strong terms (as in Matthew, although Luke omits both Peter's protestation and Christ's rebuke). This event at Caesarea Philippi is of central importance for Jesus and the disciples. It is time for them to know who Jesus is and for them to decide if they wish to continue with him.

Later, to a much larger crowd, Jesus says that discipleship means self-renunciation and indeed surrendering one's life selflessly for his sake and his teaching; only thus will a disciple of his reach salvation.

Twenty-Fifth Sunday in Ordinary Time
• Year B

Collect

Since the basis of all God's commandments is love of him and of our neighbours, we ask for the grace to obey the commandments and so reach eternal life.

First Reading   Wisdom 2:12.17-20

The book of Wisdom was composed in mid-first century BC to urge Jews to be faithful to their religion and customs despite the popularity of hellenic influences. Today's passage tells us how the godless argue in their hatred of the god-fearing. The second half of the reading is seen by Christians as foreshadowing the sufferings of Christ.

Psalm 53 (54)

The Lord upholds my life.

The psalm is a confident appeal to God for protection against dangerous enemies.

Second Reading   James 3:16-4:3

St James contrasts the virtues and good conduct that come from God's gift of wisdom with their opposites – all kinds of wickedness. In particular, wars and violence derive from our unjust desires and ambitions. If we want something, we should pray for it rather than try to get it by force; and if God does not give us what we ask for, it is because it is not good for us to have it.

Gospel   Mark 9:30-37

Today's events take place on the way from the transfiguration to Capernaum. Jesus again tells his disciples about his coming death and resurrection, but they are too bewildered to ask questions. In fact, they begin talking among themselves about which of them will be the greatest. Against this selfish mentality, Jesus rebukes and corrects the Twelve. To welcome a little child in Jesus' name (and as he himself does) is to welcome Jesus; and to welcome Jesus is to welcome the Father who sent him. In other words, it is the insignificant who are the important people in the kingdom.

Twenty-Sixth Sunday in Ordinary Time
• Year B

Collect

Acknowledging God's infinite mercy, we pray for the grace to inherit his promises of eternal life.

First Reading   Numbers 11:25-29

Numbers, the fourth book of the Pentateuch, continues the story of the Jews in the wilderness after their escape from slavery in Egypt and on their way to the Promised Land. The people often complained and grumbled and Moses told God that being the sole leader was too much for him. So God told him to select seventy elders to share his responsibility and to bring them to the tent of meeting so that he, God, could put some of the spirit that was on Moses on them too. Two of the elders had not been in the tent of meeting but they also received the spirit. This confused some of the people and they asked Moses to stop the two from prophesying. Moses refused, saying he wished that everyone had been given the spirit. [The spirit received by the elders is not explicitly the Holy Spirit, but God's breath, signifying his power and authority.]

Psalm 18 (19)

The precepts of the Lord gladden the heart.

The psalm celebrates God's wisdom and encourages us, if we wish to be virtuous, to discover and obey his decrees.

Second Reading   James 5:1-6

This final extract from the letter of James is an outright condemnation of the rich for their pitiless injustices to the poor. The punishment of the rich will come with the end times and the general judgment.

Gospel   Mark 9:38-43.45.47-48

The first half of today's gospel reading shows John telling Jesus about the disciples' desire to be the only ones allowed to do good in Jesus' name. Jesus scolds them because it is not their own prestige that matters but the care of those in need. The second half of the passage comes from various teachings of Jesus: the evil of leading others astray and three warnings about the dangers of self-ensnarement.

Twenty-Seventh Sunday in Ordinary Time
• Year B

Collect

To God, whose kindness is far beyond our expectations, we pray for forgiveness and for the gifts that only he can know and bestow.

First Reading   Genesis 2:18-24

The account in Genesis, chapter 2, of God's making of the beasts and birds and especially of the first woman. The purpose of these actions is that 'it is not good that the man should be alone' and, in particular reference to the making of the woman from a rib of the man, to provide 'a suitable helpmate' for him.

Psalm 127 (128)

May the Lord bless us all the days of our life.

This short psalm celebrates the blessings of domestic virtue. It can be considered as the consequence to be sought from the union of man and woman in marriage.

Second Reading   Hebrews 2:9-11

The first of seven excerpts from the letter to the Hebrews, sent probably around 67 AD by an unknown author to a group of Jewish Christians whom persecution had discouraged and who were in danger of reverting to Judaism.

Today's passage declares that Christ is glorified because he suffered a death which God accepted as redemptive of the human race. It was fitting, says the letter, that God should make perfect the leader and saviour who, in fact, is also the brother of those he saved.

Gospel   Mark 10:2-16

Some pharisees are 'testing' Jesus on the question of divorce, especially because Moses had apparently allowed it in certain circumstances (Deuteronomy 24:1). Jesus says that that was only because the people were so 'unteachable' (obdurate, hard-hearted, thick-headed); but now Jesus orders a return to the original rule that forbade divorce. He reiterates this teaching to the disciples.

Today's gospel passage also shows that Jesus taught the disciples that he had love and time for children and that his followers should be the same. Moreover, the manner in which children welcome the kingdom of God is the model for everyone. It is not the rich and influential who should be prominent or imitated. (Both Matthew (19:13-15) and Luke (18:15-17) describe this incident in similar words.)

Twenty-Eighth Sunday in Ordinary Time • Year B

Collect

We ask for God's grace to be always with us, urging us to help others.

First Reading   Wisdom 7:7-11

The book of Wisdom extols that gift of wisdom as far more important than anything else, whether riches and treasures or personal qualities. The author (first century BC) is using the literary subterfuge of pretending that Solomon (tenth century BC) is addressing other kings.

Psalm 89 (90)

Fill us with your love that we may rejoice.

The wise man reflects on the shortness and troubles of human life and, in the final verses which are used today, asks God for 'wisdom of heart' so that we can rejoice in true happiness, which is God's love for us and his favour.

Second Reading   Hebrews 4:12-13

The letter to the Hebrews tells us that the teachings of the prophets and of Jesus are so acute and penetrating that we cannot hide from them or avoid being laid open and judged by them. There is no escape; no one can elude them. So God will judge us by measuring us against the standards set by his word.

Gospel   Mark 10:17-30

A sad story of a young man seeking to be perfect and to be assured of eternal life. He kept the commandments but knew there was something still lacking. When Jesus tells him to sell all his possessions and give the money to the poor, he walks away. Why? Because 'he was a man of great wealth'. The affluent can be prisoners of their own material well-being with a religion that lacks practical love for the poor and the freedom and joy that come with that love.

Since wealth was generally assumed to be a sign of God's favour, the disciples are amazed when Jesus tells them that it is hard for the wealthy to enter God's kingdom. The severity of Jesus' words should not be lessened by explaining away the 'camel and eye of a needle' saying as exaggeration. But God has ways of getting even the rich into his kingdom!

The final section of today's passage may be a later addition because Jesus did not normally promise rewards in this life and even the distinction between 'now' and 'in the world to come' is unusual for Jesus; moreover, the promise of persecution seems to be in contradiction with the promise of great prosperity. The account of Jesus' response to Peter's enquiry seems awkward.

Twenty-Ninth Sunday in Ordinary Time • Year B

Collect

We ask God that we may always do his will and serve him sincerely.

First Reading   Isaiah 53:10-11

From Second Isaiah, this reading is part of the fourth 'song of the servant of the Lord'. It is clearly messianic.

Psalm 32 (33)

May your love be upon us, O Lord,
as we place all our hope in you.

Psalm 32 (33) acclaims the Lord as king of Israel and of all the nations. It rejoices in God's fidelity and providence.

Second Reading   Hebrews 4:14-16

This short excerpt from Hebrews begins a development of the meaning of Christ's priesthood, its similarities to the Jewish priesthood and its superiority. Jesus is the supreme high priest who, being human, has experienced our weaknesses and temptations. But, as he is now in heaven, our certainty of the efficacy of his work is assured. We can be confident of God's gift of salvation.

Gospel   Mark 10:35-45

Jesus and the Twelve are walking to Jerusalem. The apostles are confused and very nervous. Nevertheless, the two brothers go silently to Jesus and make their selfish request. Jesus is taken aback at their unworthy ambition. When the others get to know, they are very angry – but because they also have a similar unworthy ambition. So Jesus calls them together to rebuke and to instruct. His followers must not be like the Romans who sought power and position over others. Christians will be great only if they seek to help and serve and be available for others. For he himself 'did not come to be served but to serve'.

Thirtieth Sunday in Ordinary Time
• Year B

Collect

Asking God to increase our faith, hope and love, we also pray to be obedient to him so as to receive what he has promised.

First Reading   Jeremiah 31:7-9

Jeremiah lived in the second half of the seventh and early decades of the sixth centuries BC and was present at the fall and destruction of Jerusalem and the forced exile of many to Babylon. Today's extract is from the section of his prophecy called the Book of Consolation and refers specifically to the promise of return from exile of the northern tribes (Israel and Ephraim are mentioned) who had been deported by the Assyrians.

Psalm 125 (126)

What marvels the Lord worked for us!
Indeed we were glad.

This short psalm (used here in its entirety) is a joyful song of exiles returning home. They seek God's help in resettling and replanting the land.

Second Reading   Hebrews 5:1-6

The letter to the Hebrews again shows the similarity between Christ's high priesthood and that of the Jewish high priests. Both experienced human weakness and temptations (and, for the latter, personal sinfulness also) and both received the honour of priesthood from God. In today's reading, psalm 109/110 is quoted in the case of Jesus and, although verses 1 to 3 are also quoted of Jesus in other texts of the New Testament, this is the only New Testament text that applies verse 4 ('a priest of the order of Melchizedek') to Jesus.

Gospel   Mark 10:46-52

The healing of the blind beggar of Jericho makes very consoling reading for those with problems of sight. The desire of many to silence Bartimaeus shows their poor understanding of Jesus and his mission. Restoration of sight to the eyes is associated with reception of the gift of faith, which happened here since not only did the blind man's faith 'save' him, but he then 'followed' Jesus.

Thirty-First Sunday in Ordinary Time
• Year B

Collect

Recognising that even our service of God is his gift, we pray that we may proceed without mishap on the way to receive our promised inheritance.

First Reading   Deuteronomy 6:2-6

The book of Deuteronomy comprises discourses of Moses to the Israelites on their trek to the Promised Land and also a code of civil and religious laws. Today's short excerpt is the crucial and basic precept. It is a declaration of a monotheistic faith, one only God, whom the Jews are to obey, to fear (a son's or daughter's fear, not a slave's) and to love. The command in verses 4 and 5 is the start of the prayer still central for Jews, the *shema*, while Jesus declared it the greatest of all commandments (Matthew 22:37-38).

Psalm 17 (18)

I love you, Lord, my strength.

The psalm is a song of triumph, praising God for protection and victory. It originated as a song of thanksgiving to God by David when he was delivered from the power of his enemies and especially of King Saul.

Second Reading
Hebrews 7:23-28

This extract from the letter to the Hebrews contrasts the priesthood of the earlier Jewish high priests with that of Christ. Theirs was temporary and ended at their death; his is everlasting. They had to offer sacrifices repeatedly; Christ had to do so only once, by offering himself as victim. They offered for their own sins as well as the sins of others; Christ is sinless and perfect.

Gospel
Mark 12:28-34

Jesus had been debating with some of the religious authorities who opposed him – pharisees, Herodians, Sadducees. A scribe who had been listening was impressed by Jesus and his answers. (The scribes were persons of authority in Scripture interpretation and judicial decisions, and were members of the Sanhedrin by right.) The scribe's question to Jesus is a friendly one and he commends Jesus for his answer (which is to cite the *shema*, today's first reading from Deuteronomy, and then to add a necessary 'partner' about love of others). Jesus tells the scribe that he is very much in line with the values of God's kingdom.

Thirty-Second Sunday in Ordinary Time
• Year B

Collect

We ask our divine Father to keep us free from all obstacles of mind or body that would hinder us from seeking the things of God.

First Reading
1 Kings 17:10-16

The prophet Elijah (enemy of King Ahab and his pagan wife Jezebel who had brought idolatry of Baal to Israel in the ninth century BC) performs a miracle for a starving widow and her son. He increases the tiny quantity of flour and oil that she had left, in order to feed the three of them until 'the day when the Lord sends rain'.

Psalm 145 (146)

> *My soul, give praise to the Lord.* or *Alleluia!*

For today's responsorial psalm, we use the final verses of a psalm recited in the morning by Jews and which praises God, always ready to help those in need or misfortune.

Second Reading   Hebrews 9:24-28

Again, familiar themes from the letter to the Hebrews. Christ, our perfect high priest, enters God's presence and takes there his sacrifice for our sins, his own blood whose effects are unlimited. Just as we die only once and then face judgment, so Jesus dies only once, sacrificing himself for others' sins, and then, on his second coming, it will be as judge (with salvation for the saved).

Gospel   Mark 12:38-44

In today's gospel reading, Jesus is in Jerusalem for the Passover feast. His own passion and death are near. He is teaching in the temple precincts and observes two examples that illustrate the points he is making: first, the scribes with their hypocritical ostentation; and second, the poor widow's small but, for her, extremely generous offering to the funds for the temple worship. Jesus favours humility and poverty in his disciples.

Thirty-Third Sunday in Ordinary Time
• Year B

Collect

We ask 'the author of all that is good' to give us the happiness of being constant in our service of him.

First Reading   Daniel 12:1-3

The book of Daniel was written quite late in the Old Testament, around 165 BC, to sustain the faith of Jews, at a time of persecution, by recalling the faith of those in exile centuries earlier. The first part of the book is a narrative of Daniel and his companions, the latter part is of various visions, especially eschatological (i.e., of the end of the world). Today's passage is about the events at that time – 'a time of great distress' and destruction. Some (many) of the living will be destined for eternal life, while of those already dead, many will rise, 'some to everlasting life, others to everlasting disgrace'. It is only at this time, in the second century BC, that a belief in the resurrection of the body is clearly stated.

Psalm 15 (16)

Preserve me, God, I take refuge in you.

The psalmist believes that God is his heritage and so he expresses hope and trust that God will not allow him to cease to exist at death. Here, there is an early hint that will develop into the belief expressed in today's first reading. The psalm was seen as messianic in Judaism and, for Christians, is fulfilled in the resurrection of Christ.

Second Reading   Hebrews 10:11-14.18

Yet again, the letter to the Hebrews asserts the efficacy of Christ's self-sacrifice for our sins, compared with the sacrifices of the Old Law.

Gospel   Mark 13:24-32

Chapter 13 of Mark's gospel reports the eschatological discourse of Jesus, when he spoke about the events that would happen at the end of the world and his own second coming for the general judgment. Jesus was speaking to the apostles as they were sitting on the Mount of Olives, looking across the Kidron Valley towards the temple and the city of Jerusalem. He tells of great cosmic signs before 'the Son of Man' (as he designates himself on solemn occasions) appears in glory. Jesus adds that, just as we know that summer is near when the fig trees get their leaves, so those happenings will warn that the coming of the Son of Man is imminent. But, at this moment of speaking to the disciples, Jesus says that only the Father knows when the end time will be.

Today's passage is only a small part of chapter 13, the eschatological discourse. Other parts of it refer to the Roman army's destruction of Jerusalem following a Jewish uprising, 70 AD. So the warning in our excerpt that 'all this will have taken place in the present generation' has got more relevance for that, rather than for the end of the world.

Our Lord Jesus Christ, King of the Universe • Year B

(Thirty-Fourth Sunday in Ordinary Time)

Collect

Since it is God's will that everything be restored in his Son, King of the universe, we pray that all creation, freed from slavery, may always serve and praise God.

First Reading   Daniel 7:13-14

As last week, the first reading is from the Book of Daniel. The vision this time is of 'a son of man' (a phrase basically meaning a man but, when used as here, an exceptional person, one who is somehow more than human). A son of man is brought into the presence of 'the Ancient of Days' and given eternal and universal sovereignty. Clearly a prophecy about the messiah and eschatological times.

Psalm 92 (93)

The Lord is king, with majesty enrobed.

God's kingly sovereignty, shown by the laws imposed on the physical world and by his laws for humankind, is acknowledged and praised. His dwelling place is holy.

Second Reading   Apocalypse 1:5-8

The Apocalypse (The Book of Revelation) is often attributed to St John the Evangelist and dated around 90 AD, but both author and date are uncertain. 'Apocalypse' means a revelation from God, especially of future events and in highly symbolic language. Hence, the interpretation is often difficult and disputed. It is not easy to draw a clear distinction between prophecy and apocalypse; the former was usually God's word heard and passed on by word of mouth; the latter was a revelation revealed and passed on in writing.

This excerpt is from the introduction of the book and, using many allusions from the Old Testament, it speaks about Jesus Christ, King and Messiah, his solemn enthronement and his future reign over God's royal and priestly people. In fact, the reading summarises the content and purpose of the whole book.

Gospel   John 18:33-37

In John's gospel, Jesus, on trial before Pilate, declares that he is a king, but not of this world's kind or with military power (or as a threat to the Roman occupation of the country). He was born to bear witness to this truth of his kingship and to make this truth known to those who will listen. The gospels' accounts of Christ's years of public life show clearly that his kingship is exactly as he tells Pilate; moreover, it is a kingship of service and he is a king for all, and especially for the poor, the outcast, the powerless and the despised.

The Sunday Collects and Readings of Year C

Advent and Christmas, Year C

First Sunday of Advent • Year C

*'Advent' means 'coming' and therefore, for us, it involves a time of 'waiting'.
But this should be understood as having a sense of 'desire' and 'expectancy'.*

Collect

We pray that we may meet Jesus when he comes and that he will take us into the kingdom of God.

First Reading   Jeremiah 33:14-16

Jeremiah was born in mid-seventh century BC and was called as a prophet by God in 626. He lived through the tragic years of the ruin of the kingdom of Judah, including the fall of Jerusalem and the deportation of many to exile in Babylon. Jeremiah was among those who remained in Jerusalem but finally was taken to Egypt where he died. He was a devout man and a candid prophet.

In this passage, a better future for both Judah and Israel is foretold, with an honest descendant of David to be ruler. The passage is clearly looking forward to the messianic age.

Psalm 24 (25)

To you, O Lord, I lift up my soul.

This psalm seeks the Lord's guidance while we long, as his covenanted people, to live in accordance with his will.

Second Reading   1 Thessalonians 3:12-4:2

In this letter to the church in Thessalonika (in northern Greece), Paul urges the people to advance more and more in lives of holiness and love and to follow the instruction that he gave them while he was with them. Many Christians expected an early return of Christ and there is a hint in the text that this second coming may be near.

Gospel   Luke 21:25-28.34-36

Today we begin Year C, the 'Year of Luke'.

Chapter 21 is a mixture of accounts of the destruction of Jerusalem (AD 70) and of the second coming of Jesus. This latter is described in today's gospel passage. The language is apocalyptic (i.e., God's revelation but in symbolic language that is hard to understand and interpret) as is shown in the first part of today's excerpt; but then, in the second part, Jesus speaks of our liberation (redemption from sinfulness) and the need to be watchful and prepared.

Second Sunday of Advent • Year C

Advent is a time of waiting, but our waiting should be a 'looking forward' with joy and hope.

Collect

May God help us to be eager to meet his Son and to have the faith we need in order to be in his company.

First Reading   Baruch 5:1-9

The prophet Baruch, a disciple of Jeremiah, was writing from exile in Babylon to the Jews still in Jerusalem, hoping that the text would be read at liturgical meetings. This excerpt encourages the people of the city to rejoice because God has not forgotten them. He will restore their glory and reputation and will bring back the exiles, making the way easy for them. This passage has messianic reference and the language of the way back being made smooth is based on Isaiah (chapter 40:3-5) and is used in John the Baptist's preaching (in today's gospel).

Psalm 125 (126)

What marvels the Lord worked for us!
Indeed we were glad.

This short psalm, used today in its entirety, is a joyful song of thanksgiving to God by the exiles returned from slavery.

Second Reading   Philippians 1:3-6.8-11

Paul visited Philippi (in the Macedonian province of northern Greece) several times and had good memories of the church there. This is a friendly letter (written from prison, probably in Ephesus) in which Paul speaks of his confidence in their continuing advance in wisdom, mutual love and desire to share their faith. Again there is an eschatological reference to the 'Day of Christ'.

Gospel   Luke 3:1-6

The gospel last Sunday was from Luke's account of Christ's eschatological teaching, given at the end of his public ministry. Today the excerpt is about the preaching of John the Baptist, before the public life of Jesus had begun. The quotation from Isaiah (40:3-5) speaks about smoothing the way for God and about salvation being offered for all, not only for Jews.

Luke usefully dates his account by events in the world. Both Herod Antipas and Philip were sons of Herod the Great (the former being tetrarch of Galilee, BC 4 - AD 39). Caiaphas was high priest (AD 18 - 36) and his father-in-law, Annas, was his predecessor (AD 6 - 15). The details given by Luke were used by Dionysius Exiguus (= Wee Denis) (sixth century) to calculate when Jesus was born, but wrongly. Since Herod the Great died in 4 BC, Jesus was born earlier, between 8 and 4 BC.

['Tetrarch': a title given to a satellite prince ruling a part of the Roman Empire but under ultimate Roman jurisdiction.]

Third Sunday of Advent • Year C

'Are you the one for whom we sare waiting?' This question is still being asked today.

Collect

Looking forward to the feast of Christ's nativity, we ask God to enable us to obtain the salvation that Jesus brings and to celebrate that grace with true joy.

First Reading   Zephaniah 3:14-18

One of the twelve minor prophets (that is, with shorter writings than the four major prophets: Isaiah, Jeremiah, Ezekiel and Daniel), Zephaniah wrote mainly to warn the rulers and peoples of God's disapproval of their behaviour. However, this excerpt is a cry of hope and joy for the future messianic age when God will dwell in Israel and will bring pardon and peace.

Psalm   Isaiah 12:2-6

> *Sing and shout for joy*
> *for great in your midst is the Holy One of Israel.*

Judah will one day have returned from exile in Babylon and been reunited with Israel. This song of joy and thanksgiving to God (more psalm than prophecy) was therefore inserted here as an appropriate response. Neither its author nor its date of composition is known, but it does seem later than eighth century BC. It is used here to anticipate the joy of the coming of the messiah.

Second Reading   Philippians 4:4-7

Paul informs the Philippians that he wants them to be happy, to enjoy peace and, if they need anything, to ask God confidently for it.

Gospel Luke 3:10-18

Having proclaimed the coming of the Lord and urged the people to repent of their sins, John the Baptist gives specific details of how various people must amend their ways. He then disabuses them of any idea that he was the messiah. He, John, baptises with water and for forgiveness, but the messiah will baptise with the Holy Spirit and with fire. The meaning of 'with fire' here is unclear; perhaps to remove evil from their midst or as an eschatological dimension of Christ's baptism.

Fourth Sunday of Advent • Year C

With the feast of Christmas now only days away, today's Mass and especially the readings concentrate only on the first coming of the Lord.

Collect

This prayer, already well known to many of us, expresses our awareness of Our Lord's coming among us as man and asks God for the grace that, through his Son's passion and death, we may share in his resurrection.

First Reading Micah 5:1-4

Micah exercised his ministry in the latter half of the eighth century BC, his writings mainly foretelling destruction, judgment and punishment. But there is also hope, especially in today's extract which looks forward to the messiah to be born in Bethlehem (Ephrathah is an alternative name for the town). His mother is mentioned and he will have great power and will bring peace and security to a restored Israel.

Psalm 79 (80)

> *God of hosts, bring us back;*
> *let your face shine on us and we shall be saved.*

The psalm is a prayer to God for the restoration of Israel and the reunion of Judah and (the northern kingdom of) Israel. God is invoked as shepherd and also the owner of a vine, while there is also a plea for God's chosen one to be sent (which primarily refers to one of the kings, although it could be seen as referring to the messiah).

Second Reading Hebrews 10:5-10

The letter to the Hebrews is by an unknown author, writing in an unknown place (Alexandria? Rome?) and perhaps for a group of Jews, early converts to Christianity, who were in danger of reverting to Judaism at a time of persecution. In this excerpt, the reason for Christ's coming is expressed by the author in words quoting psalm 39 (40):6-8. The passage goes on to say that therefore the Jewish sacrifices were ineffective but the one sacrifice of Christ on Calvary makes us all sanctified.

Gospel   Luke 1:39-45

Mary, hearing that her older cousin Elizabeth is pregnant, goes to be with her. They meet and we hear Elizabeth's words of greeting and welcome (but not Mary's response in today's extract). The location is usually identified as Ein Karim, 'a few miles west of Jerusalem' but nowadays a residential suburb of the city.

Two of the phrases of Elizabeth's greeting should be kept in mind: 'the mother of my Lord' (a beautiful title) and 'she who believed' (the woman of faith, blessed because she believed). Note also that Mary, bearing Jesus with her, goes to serve and help.

The Nativity of the Lord (Mass during the night): *see page 29*

The Nativity of the Lord (Mass at dawn): *see page 30*

The Nativity of the Lord (Mass during the day): *see page 31*

The Holy Family • Year C

The Holy Family is different from every other human family. Is it realistic to present it as the model for our families?

Collect

We ask God to help us to imitate the Holy Family and to practise their virtues in the lives of our own families.

Readings 1 & 2 and the Psalm for Year A (Ecclesiasticus 3:2-6.12-14, Psalm 127 (128), Colossians 3:12-21) may be read today. See p.32. Otherwise, the alternatives below are used.

First Reading   1 Samuel 1:20-22.24-28

At the beginning of the eleventh century BC, Elkanah and Hannah, late in their marriage and by God's special providence, had a son whom they named Samuel. In gratitude, once the child was weaned, they 'made him over to the Lord for the whole of his life'. He grew up to be the last and greatest of the Judges who ruled Israel.

Psalm 83 (84)

They are happy who dwell in your house, O Lord.

A song praising God who, at home in his temple, gives happiness and pardon to pilgrims who visit him and to all who serve him there.

Second Reading   1 John 3:1-2.21-24

In his first letter, St John teaches us that God has adopted us as his children. We need never fear him if we remember his commandments: belief in Jesus and love of one another.

Gospel   Luke 2:41-52

This is the only incident known to us between the infancy of Jesus and his emergence for baptism at the Jordan, already a grown man. Three festivals (Passover, Pentecost and Tabernacles) required Jews to make a Jerusalem pilgrimage but custom allowed those living far off to comply only on Passover. Jesus was twelve years old, a year before reaching legal manhood and his bar mitzvah. 'Busy with my Father's affairs' could also be translated 'busy in my Father's house' (i.e., the temple). Either version indicates a special relationship with, and prior duty towards, God the Father. The incomprehension of Mary and Joseph indicates their ignorance of Jesus' divinity at the time.

Solemnity of Mary, the Holy Mother of God: *see page 32*

Second Sunday after the Nativity: *see page 34*

The Epiphany of the Lord: *see page 35*

The Baptism of the Lord • Year C

All four evangelists report this event, implying the importance of recording it as the start of Jesus' public ministry. What is the meaning of Jesus asking to be baptised by John?

Collect

At the baptism of Jesus, the Father declared him his beloved Son. We recall that, by baptism and the Holy Spirit, God has adopted us as his sons and daughters.

Readings 1 & 2 and the Psalm for Year A (Isaiah 42:1-4. 6-7, Psalm 28 (29), Acts 10:34-38) may be read today. See p.36. Otherwise, the alternatives below are used.

First Reading   Isaiah 40:1-5.9-11

This reading is the opening of Second Isaiah or Deutero-Isaiah, the Book of the Consolation of Israel, which assures the people that their exile in Babylon will end soon; the Lord will lead them home as he did when they escaped from Egypt and he led them through the wilderness to the Promised Land. (The Greek text of verse 3 is slightly different and reads 'A voice of one who cries in the wilderness . . .', which the gospels use to denote John the Baptist in the Judean wilderness, proclaiming the messiah.)

Psalm 103 (104)

Bless the Lord, my soul!
Lord God, how great you are!

Following the sequence of Genesis, chapter one, this psalm praises God for all the stages and varieties of creation that he made. Here, we use ten of the thirty-five verses.

Second Reading   Titus 2:11-14; 3:4-7

Writing to Titus, his follower whom he had sent to work in Crete, Paul teaches that those who live good lives will be saved. This final and greatest blessing of salvation will come to us through the grace won for us by the self-sacrifice of Jesus. Thereby, we are given the 'cleansing water of rebirth' and renewal through the Holy Spirit to allow us to inherit eternal life. (This extract from Paul's letter to Titus and read on the feast of Christ's own baptism reminds us of God's plan for our salvation, achieved through Jesus and attained by baptism and the Holy Spirit.)

Gospel   Luke 3:15-16.21-22

This is Luke's version of the baptism of Jesus. First, John the Baptist declares that not he, but someone is coming who is the Christ, the messiah (see gospel for Third Sunday of Advent).

Then the excerpt tells us that, after Jesus had been baptised, he was praying when the Holy Spirit was seen descending on him in the form of a dove and the Father's voice was heard, addressing Jesus as his beloved Son.

Lent and Easter, Year C

Ash Wednesday: see page 37

First Sunday of Lent • Year C

Collect

We pray that, by our Lenten activities, we may discover and gain the riches God has prepared for us.

First Reading

Deuteronomy 26:4-10

Deuteronomy is the fifth and final book of the Pentateuch and consists mainly of civil and religious laws. In this reading Moses is instructing the people that, when they settle in the Promised Land, they must make an offering to God of the first fruits of the soil. As they do so, they are to recite the profession of faith laid down. In it, there is an expression of gratitude to God for freeing the Jews from Egyptian slavery and leading them to their new homeland.

[The Aramaeans (whose language was Aramaic) were nomads and Jews believed themselves descended from them.]

Psalm 90 (91)

Be with me, O Lord, in my distress.

The psalm speaks of the confidence of the virtuous that God, through the ministrations of his angels, will protect them in all dangers. In the final verse, God responds with an assurance of his saving care.

Second Reading

Romans 10:8-13

Paul's letter to the Romans is a profound theological treatise on the way in which we are saved – not through our own efforts but by our faith in the redeeming death and resurrection of Jesus Christ. In today's excerpt, St Paul states this truth and then adds that salvation is not restricted only to Jew or gentile; God is not only able, but also anxious, to bring everyone to eternal life.

Gospel

Luke 4:1-13

The gospel for the first Sunday of Lent is the account of Christ's forty days of fast in the wilderness and his temptations. This being Year C, we read Luke's version. Luke makes frequent mention of the Holy Spirit, both in his gospel and in the Acts of the Apostles. Today's reading begins: 'Filled with the Holy

Spirit . . .'. Scholars think that the phrase 'in a moment of time' indicates that Jesus was not moving physically from temptation to temptation but that the temptations occurred in a vision. The temptations are not strictly of the moral order but rather are an attempt to motivate Christ wrongly for his mission: to serve his own interests; to resort to abuses, lies and injustice; to seek easy success and self-display.

Second Sunday of Lent • Year C

Collect

We pray to the Father that, having listened to his beloved Son, we may be enabled to witness the Father's glory.

First Reading   Genesis 15:5-12.17-18

In this reading from the book of Genesis, God promises the childless Abram (his name not yet changed) an innumerable number of descendants. Abram is astonished but God seals the promise with a covenant in which Abram is told that his descendants are to be given the land from the Euphrates to the borders of Egypt. Abram, as the partner in the covenant, passes between the cut halves of the animals to signify that, if he violated the agreement, he called down on himself the same fate as the animals had met. The sentence 'Abram put his faith in the Lord, who counted this as making him justified' is used by St Paul to prove that justification depends on faith and not on works; but St James, saying that faith is the reason for Abram's good conduct, emphasises that faith without works is useless.

Psalm 26 (27)

The Lord is my light and my help.

A psalm of trust. Those who live in God's company need fear nothing. The phrase 'seek his face' implies to want to know God, to live in his presence and to serve him faithfully.

Second Reading   Philippians 3:17-4:1

Paul had a warm relationship with the Christians of Philippi (a town on the north-east coast of Greece). In this excerpt, he urges them, in their lives, to imitate him and others like him. We are awaiting the return of Jesus at the end of the world, when he will transform our bodies to be like his and no longer subject to their present frailty and weakness. So, 'dear friends', he says, stay faithful.

Gospel — Luke 9:28-36

The story of the transfiguration is the gospel on each Second Sunday of Lent. This being Year C, it is Luke's version that is read. The wording is similar to Mark's and Matthew's except that Luke reveals the subject of conversation that Jesus had with Moses and Elijah (namely 'his passing which he was to accomplish in Jerusalem') and speaks of the three apostles being 'heavy with sleep'. Unlike the other two evangelists, Luke does not tell us that it was at Jesus' request that the three apostles, for the time being, told no one else what they had seen.

Third Sunday of Lent • Year C

We should keep in mind that Lent is not only a season for conversion and for getting ready for Easter, but also a time of preparation for baptism, either to be received or to be remembered with its commitment renewed.

Collect

As sinners, we ask God's mercy, acknowledging also his teaching that fasting, prayer and almsgiving are remedies for sin.

(The Readings for Year A on 3rd, 4th and 5th Sundays of Lent are appropriate for those preparing for baptism at the Easter Vigil. They should be used in parishes and communities in any year when there are to be such baptisms; they can in fact be used each year in any parish or community, if so desired. See pages 40-42.)

First Reading — Exodus 3:1-8.13-15

From the book of Exodus, the second book of the Pentateuch and the book which narrates the deliverance from Egypt, the journey through the wilderness, and the covenant between God and the Jews at Sinai. In today's passage, God reveals himself to Moses at Mount Horeb (another name for Sinai). He tells him that he is to lead the people from slavery in Egypt to the Promised Land.

Moses asks God what name he is to give when the Israelites ask who sent him to them. God answers: tell them that 'I am' (Yahweh) sent you. The word that God gives to Moses is very probably an archaic form of the verb 'to be'. God chose it either (a) because God is so transcendent that it is impossible to say more and therefore, since it does not define God, it does not give anyone any power over God (as semitic thought held); or (b) it may go some way towards a definition of God in the sense of a being with unlimited existence. No matter the reason for God's choice, the word is, for Jews, a reminder of God's loving kindness and fidelity; and, for Christians, an indication of God's transcendence which resists any attempt to define God directly.

Psalm 102 (103)

The Lord is compassion and love.

This is a psalm that expresses our praise and gratitude to God for his unconditional love. We use the opening verses of the psalm, acknowledging that God's attributes which are acclaimed were made known to us by God through Moses.

Second Reading   1 Corinthians 10:1-6.10-12

In this excerpt from the first letter to the church in Corinth, Paul cites the downfall of the Israelites resulting from their sins of idolatry on their journey to the Promised Land as a warning to Christians to avoid the same sins and errors.

[Some phrases in the passage need explanation: 'baptised into Moses' = united with him, as baptism unites us with Christ; 'ate and drank the same food and drink' = manna and water from the rock, the rock which legend said accompanied the Jews as they travelled and which Paul identifies with the already existing Son of God. Typological meanings of Old Testament events are sometimes unfairly used by New Testament writers as if the only purpose for the events had been to provide types for our instruction and warning.]

Gospel   Luke 13:1-9

Today's gospel teaches that unexpected death is not the punishment for sinfulness. We must remember that death is certain for all of us, and we should always be prepared for its coming. Yet the parable shows the patience of Jesus for sinners (whereas an actual incident regarding a fig tree, recounted in Mk 11:12-14 and Mt 21:19, shows Jesus in a harsher light).

Fourth Sunday of Lent • Year C

Collect

We ask God to help us to prepare eagerly for the celebration of the Easter mysteries.

First Reading   Joshua 5:9-12

Joshua was the successor of Moses who had died just before the Jews entered the Promised Land. Today's reading tells us that, now led by Joshua and having crossed the Jordan into the Promised Land, the Israelites kept Passover, and all days thereafter, by eating what the country produced.

[*Joshua* and *Jesus* are different forms of the same name.]

Psalm 33 (34)

Taste and see that the Lord is good.

These opening verses of the psalm praise and thank God for his unfailing help whenever we ask for it.

Second Reading   2 Corinthians 5:17-21

In this passage from the second letter to the Corinthians, St Paul assures us that God has reconciled to himself those 'in Christ'; and this is done 'through Christ' who, though sinless, took on himself our sins. Paul adds that he has been given the task of telling people about God's loving plan and of appealing to them to accept it.

Gospel   Luke 15:1-3.11-32

Jesus explains to some critical religious leaders why he seeks the company of sinners and even eats with the ritually unclean. This famous parable, which is such a consolation for us sinners, was very appropriate for the circumstances of that time. The father's pity symbolises God's mercy, the younger son is the sinner, either repentant or merely desperate, the elder son's resentment is like that of the complaining scribes and pharisees. The lesson for us is not only the father's ready pardon for his erring son, but also the unhappy behaviour of the other son, which we can so easily imitate, to our own misfortune.

Fifth Sunday of Lent • Year C

Collect

We ask God to give us the kind of love that enabled his Son to sacrifice his life for our sake.

First Reading   Isaiah 43:16-21

The book of Isaiah is usually considered as having three parts. Chapters 1 to 39 are of the eighth century BC and Isaiah is proclaiming that, as punishment for their infidelity to God, both Israel (the northern kingdom) and Judah will fall to invaders. Chapters 40 to 55 are probably of the sixth century BC and composed by a disciple of Isaiah. The nation is in exile but hopeful of returning soon to its own land. The final part (56 to 66) is composite, perhaps a sequel to the second part. The excerpt we have today (from the second part, often called Deutero-Isaiah) looks forward to the liberation of Israel from exile in Babylon.

It begins by recalling the freedom that God gave the people from captivity in Egypt and then foretells a similar liberation, this time from Babylon and across the desert of Syria (where God will provide water) and home to Palestine.

Psalm 125 (126)

What marvels the Lord worked for us!
Indeed we were glad.

This short psalm, here in its entirety, is a song of thanksgiving by the exiles returning from Babylon. They see their new freedom as possible only through God's doing.

Second Reading   Philippians 3:8-14

Writing to the church in Philippi, Paul rejoices in his knowledge of Christ the Lord, for whom he willingly surrenders everything else. Perfection in discipleship is the result not of our own efforts but comes only through faith. Paul readily admits that he is not yet perfect, but he continues to strive to be perfect and to receive the prize of life with Christ.

Gospel   John 8:1-11

Today's passage, though found now in John's gospel, is not by him. (It is not in most of the early manuscripts of John's gospel, nor is the style that of John. The unknown author is possibly Luke.) Jesus is in Jerusalem for the feast of tabernacles and he is in the precincts of the temple, preaching. As usual, some religious leaders are hostile to Jesus and wish to trap him. The significance of writing on the ground is unknown (perhaps only that, to show his lack of interest in the question, Jesus was idly drawing figures on the ground) but the outcome is twofold: Jesus is not caught in an argument and the woman is converted.

Palm Sunday of the Passion of the Lord: *see page 43*

Thursday of the Lord's Supper: *see page 44*

The Celebration of the Passion of the Lord: *see page 45*

The Easter Vigil: *see page 46*

Easter Sunday: *see page 48*

Second Sunday of Easter • Year C

It is noteworthy that the Roman Missal (2011) gives an alternative designation for this Sunday: 'The Sunday of Divine Mercy'.

Collect

We seek a deeper faith and a better appreciation of God's generous gifts to us, namely, Christ our redeemer, the Holy Spirit who gives us new life, and baptism itself by which we have access to Jesus and the Spirit.

First Reading   Acts 5:12-16

This is the third time that the Acts of the Apostles describes the early Christian community in Jerusalem. The passage stresses the miraculous power of the apostles, especially of Peter, and the increasing number both of believers and of the healed.

Psalm 117 (118)

> *Give thanks to the Lord for he is good,*
> *for his love has no end.*   or   *Alleluia, alleluia, alleluia!*

This psalm was a processional hymn for the feast of tabernacles. It is a song praising and thanking God for his goodness. The 'rejected stone' originally referred to the rebuilding of the temple, but it is seen by Christians as a messianic metaphor. The phrase which ends the middle verse is now a frequent Easter acclamation ('This day was made . . .') and we see, in the final verse, a reference to Christ ('Blessed . . . is he who comes . . .').

Second Reading   Apocalypse 1:9-13.17-19

In Year C, the second reading on Sundays in Eastertide is from the Apocalypse, also called the Book of Revelation. It probably dates from the end of the first century AD and may have been written by John the Apostle and Evangelist. Apocalyptic writing is very symbolic, not to be taken literally. To interpret it is often difficult, although it is helpful to know the historical conditions of the time at which it was written and the purpose and readers that the author had in mind.

Today's excerpt introduces the book's author, a disciple confined on the island of Patmos in the Aegean. He is instructed to write what he saw in his vision by Jesus Christ, symbolically described ('a Son of man', long robe of priesthood, golden girdle of royalty, dead and now immortal, First and Last, power to release souls from sheol).

Gospel   John 20:19-31

When risen, Jesus still has a real physical body, but no longer subject to the limitations that are present before death. In the glorified state, he can appear and disappear at will. John's gospel describes Jesus coming to where the disciples were gathered on Easter Sunday. He greets them with the customary words, proves that it is truly he, orders them to continue the work he began, breathes on them to indicate that he is giving them the Holy Spirit to empower them.

The following Sunday, Jesus makes a similar appearance but this time the encounter with the previously absent and doubting Thomas confirms the truth that the Lord is risen and alive. The gentle rebuke, and then the explanation of the reason for the gospel being written, end the account of this special appearance of the risen Lord.

Third Sunday of Easter • Year C

Collect

As we rejoice in our adoption as God's children, we look forward to even greater rejoicing at the resurrection of our bodies.

First Reading   Acts 5:27-32.40-41

The Sanhedrin was the High Court for religious and political affairs. It met twice weekly in the temple. The high priest presided and the other seventy members were representatives of the leading families, former high priests, Sadducees (descendants of Zadok the Priest) and some scribes, doctors of the law and pharisees. This reading narrates an appearance of the apostles before the Sanhedrin and their refusal to be silenced in their preaching.

Psalm 29 (30)

I will praise you, Lord, you have rescued me.   or   *Alleluia!*

This psalm gives thanks to God because, through God's grace, the author has escaped from or avoided mortal danger.

Second Reading   Apocalypse 5:11-14

The author of the Apocalypse has a vision of God ('the One sitting on the throne') and Jesus ('the Lamb') surrounded by great numbers of angels and saints as well as the four animals (=four angels who, on behalf of God, direct the world (Ezekiel 1:5-21)). The praise of Father and Son by those assembled is then taken up by all living things. (Jesus is the Passover Lamb sacrificed for our salvation.)

Gospel   John 21:1-19

This final chapter of John's gospel is usually designated an appendix, added later by the evangelist or one of his followers to the main part of the gospel, which already has a conclusion.

The appendix gives us the story of the encounter which seven of the disciples (most of them apostles, it seems) had with Jesus on the shores of the Sea of Galilee. After an unsuccessful night's fishing, the disciples are surprised by a stranger on the shore calling to them and giving directions about where there was a shoal of fish, 153 altogether. The stranger turns out to be Jesus and he cooks a meal for them. After they have eaten, there occurs the moving dialogue between Jesus and Peter ('Do you love me?' 'Yes, Lord, I do'. 'Feed my sheep'), three times to remind and forgive Peter, it is usually said, following his triple denial at the trial of Jesus. Then, lastly, Jesus prophesies that Peter would die a martyr's death ('someone will put a belt round you and lead you where you would rather not go') as the final proof that he is truly a follower of Jesus.

Today's gospel passage has an important lesson for us, expressed symbolically. Without Jesus and in the darkness, the apostles' fishing yields nothing. Only the presence and light of Christ can make evangelising work effective. We do not know either (a) why the apostles had returned to their former employment of fishing (although this chapter 21 is a later addition and seems to lack continuity with the previous narrative) or (b) what is the significance of the number of fish in the net. The dialogue between Jesus and Peter brings out once more the latter's leading place. Probably no difference need be found between 'lambs' and 'sheep'.

Fourth Sunday of Easter • Year C

Although today we pray especially for those whom God calls to the ordained priesthood and to consecrated life, do not be misled: God calls all of us who are baptised to be active and effective witnesses of his Son.

Collect

Our Good Shepherd has gone to eternal life. We ask God that the sheep of the flock may follow him there.

First Reading   Acts 13:14.43-52

The early part of the Acts of the Apostles tells the story of the first generation of Christians in Jerusalem. From chapter 13, the focus is on Paul and his work. In today's reading, Paul and Barnabas are on their first missionary journey and have reached Antioch in Asia Minor (not the Antioch in Syria). They preach with boldness and make converts, but some Jews are very hostile and succeed in having them expelled from the city.

Psalm 99 (100)

We are his people, the sheep of his flock. or *Alleluia!*

A psalm of praise and thanks to God, our Shepherd.

Second Reading   Apocalypse 7:9.14-17

This vision is of the martyrs, victims in the persecution of Nero (64 AD), now in God's presence and standing in front of the Lamb 'who will be their shepherd'.

Gospel   John 10:27-30

John's gospel, chapter 10, provides the gospel passages for this fourth Sunday of Easter in all three years, A, B and C. Jesus assumes the title of the Good Shepherd (already common in the Old Testament for God). Today, Jesus speaks of our total dependence on him for eternal life.

The claim that 'the Father and I are one' though, in itself, may mean only shared power, clearly hints at a deeper unity. As a result, the next passage, not read, speaks of Jews accusing Jesus of blasphemy.

Fifth Sunday of Easter • Year C

Collect

We ask God to bring the paschal mystery to fulfilment in us so that, after baptism, we may advance in goodness and reach eternal happiness.

First Reading   Acts 14:21-27

This excerpt from Acts describes the latter part of the first missionary journey which took Paul and Barnabas to various towns in Asia Minor before they returned to the church at Antioch in Syria.

Psalm 144 (145)

I will bless your name for ever,
O God my King. or *Alleluia!*

This psalm addresses God as a mighty and glorious King, yet also kind and merciful.

Second Reading   Apocalypse 21:1-5

In the penultimate chapter of the Apocalypse, the vision is of creation renewed and transformed. In it, the city of Jerusalem, also made new, becomes
the bride and dwelling place of God. God will live among his people who will
no longer experience death or grief. Creation, renewed, has become heaven.

Gospel   John 13:31-35

The scene is the Last Supper. Since Judas has gone to arrange the betrayal,
Jesus says that the passion (his glorification) has begun. God is glorified in Jesus
and will thus glorify Jesus in God himself. The apostles cannot go with Jesus
(not until death comes for them too) but their love for each other will be the
distinguishing mark of discipleship. This is 'a new commandment' because,
although the commandment is found in the Mosaic Law, it is now 'new' because
we have to love as Jesus himself loves us.

Sixth Sunday of Easter • Year C

Collect

May our celebration and remembrance of Christ's saving death and resurrection bring us joy and always guide our lives in accordance with what is right.

First Reading   Acts 15:1-2.22-29

In this chapter in Acts, the question of circumcision for pagan converts to
Christianity has again arisen. The Christians in Antioch (in Syria) are told by
some from Jerusalem that circumcision is required. But Paul and Barnabas ap-
pealed and the apostles sent delegates from Jerusalem to reassure the Christians
in Antioch that circumcision was not necessary. Regarding the four prohibitions,
three need explanation: to eat food sacrificed to idols is to share in idolatry;
blood symbolises life which belongs only to God; and a strangled animal still
has blood in it.

Psalm 66 (67)

Let the peoples praise you, O God;
let all the peoples praise you.   or   *Alleluia!*

A song that praises and thanks God and begs his blessing. The gentile nations
are also called to worship God since he rules the whole earth.

Second Reading   Apocalypse 21:10-14.22-23

The author of the Apocalypse describes how the vision he was given reveals the details of the new Jerusalem proclaimed last Sunday. With God and the Lamb present in it, there was no need of a temple; nor were the sun and moon required for light, since God and the Lamb provided the light of their radiance.

Gospel   John 14:23-29

At the Last Supper, the instruction continues in which Jesus is bidding farewell to his disciples. Jesus and his Father will dwell in those who love and obey him. The Holy Spirit, the Advocate, will teach them and remind them of Christ's teaching. Once again, Jesus bestows his peace on the disciples (a peace that promises salvation) and urges them to have no fear. Although he is leaving in the visible and physical sense, he will return (because the Persons of the Trinity live and act as one; and because the faith and love of the disciples will make them aware of Christ's true but mysterious presence).

The Ascension of the Lord: *see page 54*

Seventh Sunday of Easter • Year C

Collect

We believe that Jesus our Saviour is with the Father in glory and we pray that he may also and always be present with us here on earth.

First Reading   Acts 7:55-60

The deacon Stephen had already infuriated the Sanhedrin by his fearless witness, recalling the frequent infidelity of the Jews during their history. Now his vision, facilitated by the Spirit and making visible God the Father and the Son, was the last straw. Dying, he begs forgiveness for his persecutors (as did Jesus). Saul makes his entrance into the story of Christianity.

Psalm 96 (97)

The Lord is king, most high above all the earth.   or   *Alleluia!*

A psalm to celebrate the kingship of the Lord, universal and triumphant.

Second Reading   Apocalypse 22:12-14.16-17.20

The final extract from the Apocalypse and the book's closing words. Jesus, or an angel speaking in his name, promises his second coming and the general judgment. Then the Holy Spirit and the Bride (i.e., the Church) respond to Jesus, the Messiah: 'Come' ('maranatha' = 'Lord, come'). The promise is repeated and so is the response of longing and welcome.

Gospel   John 17:20-26

This is the final part of Our Lord's priestly prayer at the Last Supper (John chapter 17). In it, Jesus prays for the unity of all those who will become his disciples through the preaching of the apostles. The prayer then ends with Christ asking the Father to keep his disciples close to him (Jesus), to continue to deepen their faith, to love them and to enable him to be in them.

Pentecost Sunday: *see page 57*

The Most Holy Trinity • Year C

The Trinity is the most mysterious of all mysteries, totally beyond our compre-hension. However, God has revealed some aspects of the mystery. We should be anxious to know these aspects as well as venerating and adoring the one God of three Persons, equal in eternity and majesty.

Collect

As God revealed the mystery of the Trinity by sending into our world the divine Word and the Holy Spirit, we pray that we may believe with faith that God is one in nature but three distinct Persons, Father, Son and Spirit.

First Reading   Proverbs 8:22-31

In the Old Testament, the idea of Wisdom is gradually developed. In this passage from the book of Proverbs, composed after the return from exile and when the danger of polytheism had receded, Wisdom is personified as created before all other creatures, God's partner in the work of creation, and now with humans, leading us to God. Later Old Testament writing seems to give Wisdom a share in God's own nature and this is fulfilled in the New Testament where Wisdom is identified with Christ, the Son of God. In the Prologue of his gospel, St John identifies Wisdom and the qualities attributed to it with the Word of God. ('In the beginning was the Word, and the Word was with God, and the Word was God'.)

[Liturgy sometimes identifies Wisdom with Mary because she collaborates with the Redeemer as it is said to do with the Creator.]

Psalm 8

How great is your name, O Lord our God,
through all the earth!

God is praised for his work of creation; and while we are grateful that God created humans also, there is a sense of wonder that we have the power to rule all creation. We must remember that this power to rule is to be exercised as stewardship.

Second Reading   Romans 5:1-5

A short but dense passage explaining the activity of the Trinity. Paul tells us that, through Christ and with faith, we know of our friendship with God and can hope for the glory that God will give. Indeed, through our present sufferings, we gain patience, through patience we gain perseverance, which brings hope. That hope is a sure hope because the Holy Spirit, given to us not merely as 'gifts' to use but as a principle of new life in us, brings to us God's love for us.

Gospel   John 16:12-15

At the Last Supper, Jesus speaks of the Spirit who will come to develop and increase our knowledge of God's revelation. The one divine revelation has its origin in the Father, it is entrusted to the Son to communicate, and brought to our full awareness by the Spirit.

The Most Holy Body and Blood of Christ • Year C

Although Holy Thursday and the Mass of the Lord's Supper solemnly commemorate Christ's gift of the Eucharist, our awareness that the following day is Good Friday overshadows our celebration that day of the Eucharist's institution. So this feast was inaugurated in the thirteenth century, first in Liége and then throughout the world. Pope Urban IV commissioned St Thomas Aquinas to compose the texts for the feast; they include the hymns Lauda Sion *and* Pange Lingua *(the final two verses of which are sung at Benediction:* Tantum ergo Sacramentum).

Collect

On this feast, the opening prayer is addressed to God the Son. We pray to him that we may be so devoted to the sacred mystery of the Eucharist that we may receive the graces won by him in his work of salvation.

First Reading   Genesis 14:18-20

Melchizedek, priest king of Salem (a place usually identified as Jerusalem) makes a sudden, brief and mysterious appearance as Abram returns victorious from battle. He offers bread and wine to Abram and receives tithes from him. Psalm 109/110 sees him as a figure of a future messiah (and Hebrews chapter 7 links him with Christ and his priesthood). Melchizedek is a priest prior to the Levitical priesthood which was inherited; his priesthood is not a family inheritance; he receives tithes from the father of God's chosen people; he offers Abraham bread and wine, prefiguring the Eucharist (as well, perhaps, as the eucharistic sacrifice since a priest's work is to offer sacrifice).

Psalm 109 (110)

You are a priest for ever,
a priest like Melchizedek of old.

This psalm acclaims a future messiah as universal king and eternal priest, properties conferred not by earthly powers or inheritance but by God himself, as were the kingship and priesthood of Melchizedek. (The New Testament and Christian tradition also accept the first verse as a prophecy of Christ's ascension.)

Second Reading   1 Corinthians 11:23-26

St Paul criticises the behaviour of Corinthian Christians when, on some occasions, they gather to celebrate the Eucharist. In the midst of his remarks, we find this description of the institution of the Eucharist at the Last Supper - the earliest biblical account, c.57 AD.

Gospel   Luke 9:11-17

All four gospels include an account of this first miracle of the multiplication of the loaves. Luke tells us that, after the Twelve returned from the mission of preaching and healing on which Jesus sent them, he took them to a lonely place near Bethsaida (on the north shore of the Sea of Galilee) to be by themselves for a while. But the crowds discovered where they were and so Jesus' plan for a period of quiet was abandoned. After Jesus had preached and healed and as evening approached, the miracle took place. John's gospel (chapter 6) uses this miracle as an introduction to the discourse which Jesus gave about himself as the 'bread of life', a gift which comprises both his teaching and holy communion.

Sundays 2-34 in Ordinary Time, Year C

Second Sunday in Ordinary Time • Year C

Collect

We ask God the all-powerful to give peace to the world.

First Reading
Isaiah 62:1-5

The later part of the book of Isaiah dates from the years when it was clear that the Babylonian exile was ending and the people were preparing to return to their homeland. This reading looks forward, in enthusiastic and poetic terms, to the glorious restoration of Jerusalem.

Psalm 95 (96)

Proclaim the wonders of the Lord
among all the peoples.

This psalm is a song honouring God as universal king and just judge.

Second Reading
1 Corinthians 12:4-11

Today and for six further Sundays, the second reading is from the last four chapters of St Paul's first letter to the church in Corinth. Earlier chapters are found in Year A (weeks 2-8) and Year B (weeks 2-6). Paul wrote three letters in all to Corinth, but the earliest is lost. All were written after he had spent eighteen months in the city (50 - 52 AD), the two extant letters dating from 57 AD. Corinth was a seaport with many problems of immoral behaviour and the letters deal with issues that had arisen for the Christians there.

In today's reading, Paul teaches that, since the community has many services to carry out, there are many gifts received, different ones to different people, but all gifts are from the Spirit and all are for God's purposes.

Gospel
John 2:1-11

We hear today of the first public miracle of Jesus (recounted in John's gospel). Mary is present, as she was also on Calvary, at the end of his public life. It is at her request that Jesus performs the miracle, although reluctantly because the hour (of his glorification) lay ahead (this being a prophetic anticipation of it). Consequently, the miracle allows his future glory to be seen here. The miracle is called a sign (the first), since Jesus performed miracles as a sign of his divine mission.

Third Sunday in Ordinary Time • Year C

Collect

The opening prayer asks the Father to guide us so that all our activities may be done in the name of Jesus and be pleasing to God.

First Reading   Nehemiah 8:2-6.8-10

The book of Nehemiah was written in the third century BC but tells of events in the sixth century BC when the Jews were allowed to return from exile in Babylon to Jerusalem, to rebuild the temple and eventually, despite Samaritan opposition, to repair the city walls. Nehemiah is the high commissioner, answerable to the (then) Persian governor. Ezra is the scribe who reads (from the Pentateuch) the Law of Moses to the assembly and the people promise to observe it. Then the great feast of tabernacles (a harvest festival and also with some historical and religious commemorations) is celebrated with rejoicing.

Psalm 18 (19)

Your words are spirit, Lord,
and they are life.

This part of the psalm celebrates God as the source and author of the law, which therefore has to be obeyed not only in what we say but even also in our thoughts.

Second Reading   1 Corinthians 12:12-30

Paul teaches the Corinthians (and us) that we all, though many and diverse and with different gifts, make up the one ('mystical') body of Christ. And, just as a human body, with its many different parts, is one, so also is Christ. The analogy of society as a human body with many different parts is a classical comparison but, for Paul, was probably made more acute because, at his conversion and after being an enemy of Christians (many in number), he was told 'I am Jesus whom you are persecuting'. Today's passage goes on to say that, just as the parts of the body have different purposes and status but form a unity, so in Christ we have different gifts and ministries with their own varied importance, but all of us are united as one.

Gospel   Luke 1:1-4; 4:14-21

We now begin our weekly gospel readings from Luke's narrative of the Lord's public ministry. After an introduction of himself by the evangelist, Luke tells us that, after his baptism and period in the desert, Jesus ('with the power of the Spirit in him') returned to Galilee and indeed to Nazareth where he had lived his hidden youth and there he reads aloud in the synagogue the messianic prophecy in (the third part of) Isaiah (61:1-2). The prophecy is not about a more perfect religion or more solemn worship but about 'a preferential option for the poor'. He then announces to the people that, before their very eyes, that prophecy is being fulfilled at that precise moment. He is the one to whom Isaiah was referring. ['Nazara' is an uncommon variation of 'Nazareth'.]

Fourth Sunday in Ordinary Time • Year C

Collect

We pray to be able to give God genuine honour and to have a sincere love for everyone.

First Reading   Jeremiah 1:4-5.17-19

The prophet Jeremiah lived in and near Jerusalem throughout his life, which spanned the second half of the seventh century BC and the early decades of the sixth. He was devout, dedicated to the mission God gave him and, since he lived in very troubled times (immorality, idolatry, war, invasion, fall and destruction of Jerusalem and the temple), his words are often about God's displeasure and warnings of impending punishment and disaster.

This reading comes from the opening chapter of Jeremiah, relating his call and his difficult mission which will bring opposition and suffering to him; but God will protect and strengthen him to be courageous and faithful in the work he has to do.

Psalm 70 (71)

My lips will tell of your help.

This psalm speaks of God's protection over a long life and implores God to continue his guidance and protection. The psalm could be the prayer of an individual or even of the nation of Israel.

Second Reading   1 Corinthians 12:31-13:13

This famous chapter 13 of Paul's first letter to the church in Corinth occurs after Paul had explained that God gives many gifts to enable us to fulfil his plans; and, since we have differing work to do, we receive different gifts.

However, there is one gift that is the best of all and which God offers to everyone – the gift of love/charity/agape. It is a copy of God's love for us, having no possessiveness or desire for personal satisfaction, but is solely for the good of the other. At the end, Paul lists the three so-called theological virtues which he frequently cites in his letter, not always in the same order but seen as basic if we wish to be disciples of Christ.

Gospel   Luke 4:21-30

The mood changes in the synagogue at Nazareth, from admiration to hostility. Luke has, in fact, been describing two (or perhaps three) different occasions when Jesus was in Nazareth. In the present case, Jesus had been working in and from Capernaum and he bluntly tells the people of Nazareth why: they have little faith.

Jesus was not a priest of the temple nor a teacher of the Law, but a prophet, and so not legally authorised but sent by God to criticise injustices and to call for conversion.

Fifth Sunday in Ordinary Time • Year C

Collect

The prayer asks for God's care and protection so that, in all matters, we may be kept safe.

First Reading   Isaiah 6:1-8

In the year 740 BC, Isaiah received his call to be a prophet. He had to proclaim the fall of Israel (the northern kingdom) and Judah (in the south) as punishment for their infidelity. This reading recounts the vision Isaiah had of God, of his own unworthiness, of his sins removed and then of his readiness to be God's messenger or prophet.

Psalm 137 (138)

Before the angels I will bless you, O Lord.

This psalm expresses deep gratitude to God for his faithful and loving care.

Second Reading   1 Corinthians 15:1-11

Paul tells the Corinthians that they must continue to believe what he taught them while he was with them. He then reminds them of Christ's death, resurrection and subsequent appearances. Several of these appearances that Paul mentions raise questions. For example, he cites one to 'more than five hundred brothers' and another to James, neither of which are mentioned in the gospel accounts. And the appearance to 'all the apostles': is this different from 'the Twelve'? Appearances to women are omitted, perhaps because in Jewish law they would not be accepted as responsible witnesses. The appearance of Jesus to Paul on the road to Damascus is not differentiated from the pre-ascension appearances in the gospels.

Gospel   Luke 5:1-11

Today's gospel passage from Luke describes the early days of Jesus' ministry. He preaches, uses Simon's boat, helps him to a large catch, hears Simon confess that he is a sinner, and then calls him, Andrew, James and John to leave their boats and nets to work with him. Luke has Jesus preaching before calling the disciples while, for Mark, the reverse is the case. It is suggested that perhaps Luke wanted to make their unhesitating response seem less surprising.

Sixth Sunday in Ordinary Time • Year C

Collect

We ask God to make our hearts fit places for him to dwell in.

First Reading   Jeremiah 17:5-8

Jeremiah includes two contrasting pieces of wise advice. To put one's trust in human help or material things is foolish; while to put one's trust in God will assure help and success.

Psalm 1

Happy the man who has placed
his trust in the Lord.

This first of the 150 psalms is an introduction and a summary of the moral teaching of the psalter. The lesson of the psalm is exactly the same as today's first reading to which it corresponds, except that the order is reversed: first, the wise way; then the unwise.

Second Reading   1 Corinthians 15:12.16-20

Paul's purpose in recalling Christ's resurrection now becomes evident. He sees it as the decisive proof of our future resurrection, a belief that has been slowly and gradually growing in the Old Testament. The risen Christ is called the first fruits since he is not only the herald but also the cause of our resurrection. 'For, if the dead are not raised, Christ has not been raised'. (Paul does not consider the possibility of the soul's immortality without the resurrection of the body.)

Gospel   Luke 6:17.20-26

This is the inaugural discourse of Jesus, as reported by Luke in a much shorter way than Matthew. Matthew has Jesus going up a hill; for Luke, he comes down (not necessarily all the way). Both gospels note that a crowd was present, Luke giving more details of its composition. Matthew has eight beatitudes, Luke four.

The understanding of the beatitudes also differs. Where Matthew presents them as a formula for a moral life and promising rewards in heaven, Luke presents them as unfortunate material conditions (poor, hungry, weeping, hated) to be reversed in heaven. Then Luke has four 'curses': four states of apparent good fortune now (wealthy, well fed, complacent, esteemed) which will be reversed in the next life.

Seventh Sunday in Ordinary Time • Year C

Collect

A straightforward prayer in which we ask God that all that we say and do may be pleasing to him.

First Reading   1 Samuel 26:2.7-9.12-13.22-23

In this story from the first book of Samuel, Samuel is dead, Saul is king and David has been chosen by Samuel to be Saul's successor. David is more popular with the people, Saul becomes jealous and is anxious to kill David, who therefore flees. Circumstances then put Saul in mortal danger from David who, however, spares him because the king is God's anointed (see p.10).

Psalm 102 (103)

The Lord is compassion and love.

This psalm extols God for his loving kindness. In particular, it praises and thanks God for his readiness to forgive all our sins.

Second Reading   1 Corinthians 15:45-49

Continuing his teaching on our future resurrection, Paul distinguishes between the soul (psyche) and the spirit (pneuma), the former being what gives life to animals and the human body; the latter divinises a human life, begun in this world by the gift of the Holy Spirit and completed after death. To all who are united to the risen Christ, the resurrection of the body is brought about by the Holy Spirit or by the divine principle (which God withdrew from us because of Adam's sin (Genesis 6:3)). Thereupon, the body becomes incorruptible and immortal.

Gospel   Luke 6:27-38

Luke's gospel has Jesus, immediately after giving his teaching about the beatitudes, continuing with today's lessons, viz., we must love even those who dislike us or want to hurt us, treating them with kindness and generosity; neither judging nor condemning anyone but always pardoning those who wrong us. 'Treat others as you would like them to treat you'.

[The New Testament teaches that our love should be 'agape' (for the benefit of the other) rather than 'eros' (for our own advantage).]

Eighth Sunday in Ordinary Time • Year C

Collect

A prayer for God's peace throughout the world and, in particular, that the Church may enjoy that gift.

First Reading   Ecclesiasticus 27:4-7

The book of Ecclesiasticus (or 'of Ben Sira'), was produced in the second century BC to uphold the Jewish faith and culture against Greek pagan influence. In today's brief extract, the author speaks of the importance of a person's talk as the best sign of a person's worth.

Psalm 91 (92)

It is good to give you thanks, O Lord.

This psalm praises the goodness and love of God and rejoices in the virtue of those who remain close to him.

Second Reading   1 Corinthians 15:54-58

This extract tells us that, when we become immortal at our resurrection, death and its cause, sin, are destroyed. (Here, Paul says 'Then the words of Scripture will come true'. Scripture scholars cite Isaiah 25:7-8 and Hosea 13:14 as Paul's justification for his statement.) Sin is the consequence of trying to obey the Law of Moses but our victory over sin comes by faith in Christ. So, urges St Paul, we must keep doing the Lord's work, always confident of ultimate success.

Gospel   Luke 6:39-45

Using a couple of examples of the futility of the blind leading the blind, Jesus says that anyone wishing to teach must himself be knowledgeable and competent. Similarly, just as good fruit will come only from a good tree, goodness can come only from a good person. [In today's extract from Luke, Jesus is speaking to his disciples but in Matthew's gospel (15:14 and 12:33-35) he is speaking to pharisees!]

Ninth Sunday in Ordinary Time • Year C

Collect

We ask God, in his providence, to grant us what will be for our benefit and to keep from us whatever may harm us.

First Reading   1 Kings 8:41-43

The first book of Kings treats of the death of King David and the reign of his son Solomon (tenth century BC). However, today's reading is an insertion of the sixth century BC, after the Jews returned from exile in Babylon. It is a prayer to God that any gentile who comes to pray in the temple which Solomon built will be granted his petition and that all humankind may come to know and worship the one true God.

Psalm 116 (117)

> Go out to the whole world
> and proclaim the Good News.   or   Alleluia!

This is the shortest psalm in the psalter. It is a call for all peoples to worship the one, true and faithful God. [It is the *Adoremus*, familiar as a hymn at Benediction.]

Second Reading   Galatians 1:1-2.6-10

For six Sundays, the second readings will be from St Paul's letter to the Christians of Galatia, deep in Asia Minor. It is the area where Iconium (now Konya), Lystra and Derbe are situated, towns which Paul visited on each of his three missionary journeys. The letter dates probably from AD 57 - 58 when Paul was in Corinth.

In the letter (similar to the letter to the Romans), Paul teaches that the Jewish Law of Moses had limited value because it did not provide the spiritual power to obey it. On the other hand, anyone united to Christ by faith and sharing the life of the Spirit is made perfect gratuitously and can live as God wants us to live. The Mosaic Law was good but only as a stage towards the perfection available through Christ; and it was the widespread Jewish failure to see this that allowed the gentiles to be invited. One day in the future, all Jews will discover the truth. In this first extract, Paul warns the Christians of Galatia not to follow the Judaizers, i.e., those who wanted them to incorporate some of the laws of Moses, notably circumcision, in their beliefs and practice.

Gospel   Luke 7:1-10

Jesus cures the son of the centurion. The miracle is also reported in Matthew

(8:5-10) and probably also in John (4:46-54) but with differences in the details. Two points to be noted. First, it was pleasing to the early Christians to hear of Jesus performing wonders only by his word and without being present to the person involved. Second, Jesus heaps praise on the centurion, a gentile, for his outstanding faith.

Tenth Sunday in Ordinary Time • Year C

Collect

We pray that God, the source of all that is good, may guide us to discern and do what is right.

First Reading   1 Kings 17:17-24

As last Sunday, the reading is from the first book of the Kings, but this time in the reign of Ahab, king of the northern kingdom of Israel (874 - 853 BC). Ahab's great adversary was the prophet Elijah who condemned him for introducing the worship of Baal into Israel, a sin which Elijah said was punished by a severe drought. Elijah did not leave any writings but many of his sermons and sayings, especially his condemnation of idolatry, are preserved as well as the wonders God worked through him. The raising of the widow's son to life is one such miracle.

Psalm 29 (30)

> *I will praise you, Lord,*
> *you have rescued me.*

The psalm gives thanks and praise to God for deliverance from great danger.

Second Reading   Galatians 1:11-19

Paul is aware that many Galatian Christians have been influenced by the Judaizers whose teaching is not acceptable. So Paul insists that his teaching comes directly revealed to him by Jesus Christ. Though originally a persecutor of Christians, he has now been chosen by God to preach the Good News of salvation through Christ to the gentiles. Paul gives other details of his life to show that his commission to the gentiles did not have a human origin.

Gospel   Luke 7:11-17

The miracle of the raising of the widow's son to life is told only in Luke. He places it immediately before John the Baptist sends messengers to find out whether Jesus is, or is not, the awaited messiah (an incident that is omitted from the Sunday gospels of Year C, the Year of Luke).

Eleventh Sunday in Ordinary Time • Year C

Collect

Admitting our inability to do anything good without God's help, we ask for the grace to be obedient in both intention and deed.

First Reading   2 Samuel 12:7-10.13

The second book of Samuel is principally about the reign of King David after the death of King Saul. The background to today's extract is that David had committed adultery with Bathsheba, the wife of Uriah, a soldier in the army of David. Bathsheba conceives a child. David contrives to have Uriah killed in battle by having him put in a place of great danger and then abandoned there. Thus David is able to take Bathsheba as his wife. Nathan the prophet, in God's name, accuses David of gravely sinning and tells him that God will punish him but that his sin is forgiven.

Psalm 31 (32)

Forgive, Lord, the guilt of my sin.

One of the seven 'penitential psalms'. God forgives a sinner who repents, kindness for which we are grateful and rejoice.

Second Reading   Galatians 2:16.19-21

Some of the Galatian converts had been persuaded to resume trust in, and practice of, the Mosaic Law. Paul says that their conduct is wrong and that faith in Christ, who died and rose to bring us salvation, has superseded that Law.

Gospel   Luke 7:36-8:3

Luke alone relates the story of the sinful woman when Jesus was the guest of Simon, a pharisee. Simon shows some favourable interest in Jesus by inviting him, but at the same time he is scandalised by the kindness his guest shows to a known sinner. Jesus explains his conduct. The love she has shown Jesus is because her sins have been forgiven. If her sins had not been pardoned she would not have shown such feelings of love. Then Jesus tells her that it was her faith that saved her, i.e., that resulted in her sins being forgiven.

The gospel passage ends with a summary of Jesus' lifestyle and practice. With a group, both of apostles and of devout women whom Jesus had healed, he went from town to town and village to village, preaching and proclaiming that the kingdom of God was being established.

Twelfth Sunday in Ordinary Time • Year C

Collect

Confident of God's continuing guidance, we pray that we may always live faithful to him.

First Reading   Zechariah 12:10-11; 13:1

The second half of Zechariah comes from the end of the fourth century BC. It is a disordered collection of pieces, some from earlier books, some apocalyptic and of unknown author or compiler. Today's reading is from this section and speaks, apparently, of the messianic age of kindness and prayer for Jerusalem and Judah, but also of mourning for someone who is 'pierced'.

Psalm 62 (63)

For you my soul is thirsting,
O God, my God.

The psalm expresses a deep longing for God as past divine love and help are recalled.

Second Reading   Galatians 3:26-29

Everyone who has faith in Christ and is baptised has become a child of God, whether Jew or gentile, slave or free, man or woman. As such, all are the heirs promised by God to Abraham, whose posterity is not limited to Jews.

Gospel   Luke 9:18-24

Although in general Luke follows Mark's narrative, at this point he omits a large part of it (Mark 6:45-8:26). In addition, the Sunday lectionary omits a considerable section of Luke (8:4-9:17).

Today's gospel relates a crucial point in the relationship between Jesus and the apostles – he asks them who they think he is. Peter responds with a profession of faith – 'the Christ of God', very similar to the response given in Mark, simpler than in Matthew. Jesus (calling himself the Son of Man) then foretells his future suffering, death and resurrection. Luke does not report (as Mark and Matthew do) Peter's protest and Jesus' rebuke to him. Today's gospel ends with Jesus declaring that, to be his followers, we must carry our cross daily and even surrender our lives for his sake.

Thirteenth Sunday in Ordinary Time
• Year C

Collect

We pray that God, our Father by adoption, may keep us from the darkness of error and ensure that we always walk in the light of truth.

First Reading   1 Kings 19:16.19-21

In this episode from the first book of Kings, the prophet Elijah is told by God to make Elisha his successor. For Elijah to throw his cloak over Elisha is to claim rights and authority over him. Elisha, by destroying his plough and oxen, renounces his former way of life. (Elijah's remark 'Go back . . .' is not a rebuke and perhaps means only 'Do so; I am not stopping you'.)

Psalm 15 (16)

O Lord, it is you who are my portion.

The psalmist expresses such faith and commitment to God that he pleads that the union between them may never be broken. There is therefore a vague hope and a stirring of a belief in resurrection. The psalm was seen as messianic even in pre-Christian times.

Second Reading   Galatians 5:1.13-18

Paul again urges the Galatians not to revert to the 'slavery' of the Mosaic Law. Nonetheless, freedom can lead to egoism which is contrary to the basic law towards others: 'Love your neighbour as yourself'. So, as a safeguard, we must seek to be guided by the Holy Spirit.

Gospel   Luke 9:51-62

Luke puts the whole of the rest of Our Lord's public ministry (chapters 9-21) within the framework of a journey to Jerusalem to suffer, die, rise and ascend. Most travellers from Galilee to Jerusalem avoided Samaria because of the hostility of the people there. The three encounters (actual or invented) with would-be followers are meant to illustrate the demands of discipleship. The first is told that there is no security or comfortable wellbeing; the second that nothing is more urgent (a point which Jesus makes with a play on words: let the spiritually dead bury the physically dead); and the third that there is to be no looking back or retaining ties with the past.

Fourteenth Sunday in Ordinary Time • Year C

Collect

Recognising that our fallen world was raised up through Christ's humble acceptance of suffering, we pray that we may experience the lasting joy that our rescue from sin brings us.

First Reading
Isaiah 66:10-14

The reading is from the third and final part of Isaiah, after the return from exile and therefore sixth century BC. It looks forward in apocalyptic form to a time when a renewed Jerusalem will, by God's providence, give birth and sustenance to a new nation.

Psalm 65 (66)

Cry out with joy to God all the earth.

The psalm is a glad cry to acclaim God's loving kindness to his people.

Second Reading
Galatians 6:14-18

In this final extract from the letter to the church in Galatia, Paul once again asserts that it is through faith in the death and resurrection of Jesus that we are saved. Thus we are 'the Israel of God', i.e., the true Israel, the Christian community. The letter ends with a stern warning.

Gospel
Luke 10:1-12.17-20

Jesus chooses and sends out seventy-two disciples to the places he would later go. They are to prepare the people for his visit. He gives them instructions about how they would travel, how they would seek accommodation and what they would do, both in places where they were welcomed and in places where they were not. On their return, the missionaries rejoice with Jesus on the success achieved, but he adds that they should rejoice even more that God's favour is with them.

Fifteenth Sunday in Ordinary Time • Year C

Collect

The light which God gives maintains us in the truth or restores us to it; so we pray that, by God's help, all Christians may remain faithful to Christ and his teaching.

First Reading Deuteronomy 30:10-14

As the Jews approach the Promised Land at the end of their years in the desert after their escape from Egypt, Moses, their leader, addresses them. In this excerpt from his discourse (in the book of Deuteronomy), he tells them that the Book of the Law is accessible to them and that it contains all the laws and commandments which they have to observe. Moses declares that 'the Word is very near to you'. This is the first time that the term 'Word' is used of God's personal contact with his people. The term is developed in the Wisdom books of the Old Testament and reaches fulfilment in St John's gospel where it is identified with God the Son, God made man, distinct from the Father but not a separate God.

Today, there is a choice of responsorial psalms.

1. Psalm 68 (69)

Seek the Lord, you who are poor,
and your hearts will revive.

The first two stanzas are the lament of an individual in serious trouble or danger and his appeal for God's help. The final two are a confident appeal for God's protection and liberation for the people, specifically those of Judah, as they hope to rebuild the cities of their homeland.

2. Psalm 18 (19)

The precepts of the Lord
gladden the heart.

This psalm celebrates God as the source and author of the law. The verses used today contain a reflection on God's precepts, acclaiming the benefits of the law.

Second Reading Colossians 1:15-20

This is the first of four extracts from Paul's letter to the church in Colossae, a town in Asia Minor (now Turkey in Asia). The problem there was speculation about celestial or cosmic powers, speculation that threatened the supremacy of Christ. Paul does not deny the existence of these powers but links them with the angels of Jewish tradition and makes them subordinate to Christ in the work of salvation. He also develops his teaching on our union with Christ; Christ is the head and we are the members of his mystical body. We derive life from him, the head. Today's reading is a formal instruction that brings out both these ideas - Christ is supreme over all created things and he is the head of his body, the Church. Christ is 'the first-born of all creation' in the sense that, in his created human nature, he has been given the first place of honour. Paul adds that, in addition, Christ is head and first of the saved, the first to rise from the dead and the leader of all the saved.

Gospel   Luke 10:25-37

Jesus commends the lawyer (and expert in the Mosaic Law) for his awareness of the two great commandments of love (despite the lawyer's question to
Jesus having been somewhat hostile in intention). To the lawyer's supplementary
question, 'Who is my neighbour?', Jesus replies with the parable of the Good
Samaritan. Note that the point of the parable is not only the care and help given
but also the identity of the carer – not a religious Jew but a Samaritan, an alien,
a heretic (in Jewish eyes) and a person whom Jews regarded with contempt.

Sixteenth Sunday in Ordinary Time • Year C

Collect

We ask God to be generous with his gifts and graces and pray that, with faith,
hope and love, we may be more ready to obey him.

First Reading   Genesis 18:1-10

God has already changed Abram's name to Abraham because he is to be the
father of a great nation; and he has already also entered into a covenant with
Abraham and his descendants (the sign of the covenant being circumcision).
In this reading today, three men appear to Abraham in a vision. The text is
vague about 'three' or 'one' but, if the former, it seems that one is God and
the others are angels. Abraham and Sarah offer hospitality and are told that,
when another visit takes place a year later, Abraham and Sarah, despite their
advanced years, will have a son.

Psalm 14 (15)

The just will live in the presence of the Lord.

Those who will be friends of God are those who live good lives, who observe
the moral precepts of the Commandments.

Second Reading   Colossians 1:24-28

In this part of the letter to the Colossians, Paul speaks of his suffering in
carrying out his mission. He is not suggesting that Christ's sufferings were
inadequate but that, as continuing Christ's work, he will also share in his sufferings. He then speaks of the mystery that had been hidden but is now revealed,
namely that gentiles too, though pagans, were called to salvation through union
with Christ. Salvation is not restricted to Jews.

Gospel   Luke 10:38-42

Jesus had become friendly with the two sisters, Martha and Mary (not Mary Magdalene) and their brother Lazarus, who lived in Bethany, just east of Jerusalem, on the other side of the Mount of Olives. Although most of his public work was carried out in Galilee, he visited them when he was in Judea. The point of his response to Martha's complaint is that 'few things are needed' in the material sense, specifically preparation of the meal, but that, in the spiritual sense, only one is necessary – to listen to the word of God. Jesus is explaining, rather than scolding. He speaks affectionately to her ('Martha, Martha'), but says that too much activity in the material sense can cause inner turmoil and distract us from the more important things.

Seventeenth Sunday in Ordinary Time • Year C

Collect

We seek God's protection and his guidance to use wisely the things of this world as helps that will enable us to cling to the things that last.

First Reading   Genesis 18:20-32

From the Book of Genesis, Abraham is with God and the two others (men/angels). God plans to destroy Sodom and Gomorrah on account of their sin. Abraham intercedes. Eventually, God concedes that, if there are only ten just men in Sodom, he will spare the city. The issue is: Must the good suffer along with, and because of, the wicked? At that early stage, the principle of collective responsibility was very strong while the principle of individual responsibility came only later. We know that, in Christ, God was to accept the suffering of only one man to save us all.

Psalm 137 (138)

On the day I called,
you answered me, O Lord.

God is thanked because of his love for us and his unfailing readiness to come to our assistance.

Second Reading   Colossians 2:12-14

Paul likens our baptism to going into the tomb with Jesus and then rising with him to new life (a comparison that is more evident in baptism by total immersion). The debt we had to pay for our sins was death (and the Law of Moses was unable to cancel it). But God decided that the death of his own Son would cancel the punishment for everyone else. Paul says that the charges against us and the sentence of death were 'nailed to the cross' and thus annulled.

Gospel
Luke 11:1-13

Jesus teaches his disciples to pray and, specifically, the Lord's Prayer. Luke's version is considerably different from Matthew's, omitting two petitions ('Your will be done on earth . . .' and 'Deliver us from evil'). Therefore they probably derive from different traditions, Matthew's seeming more Jewish, Luke's more Christian. Using two parables, Jesus goes on to encourage us to be insistent in our prayers of petition, the reason not being to guarantee that the object sought will always be granted but to show trust in God's continual fatherly concern. 'Ask . . . search . . . knock . . .': the first needs humility, the second a readiness to be also active, the third boldness. Jesus adds that, if a human father will give good things when asked, our divine Father will give the Spirit, the best of all good things.

Eighteenth Sunday in Ordinary Time • Year C

Collect

With loving trust we ask God to repair what we have damaged of his creation and to save it from further harm.

First Reading
Ecclesiastes 1:2; 2:21-23

The book of Ecclesiastes, though ostensibly written by Solomon, is of the third century BC. It speaks of the emptiness and futility of human things and worldly pursuits. This reading is a typical example of the general theme.

Today, there is a choice of responsorial psalms.

1. Psalm 89 (90)

O Lord, you have been our refuge
from one generation to the next.

A reflection on the shortness of life, made even shorter by sin. This is followed by a trusting cry for God's help.

2. Psalm 94 (95)

O that today you would listen to his voice!
Harden not your hearts.

This psalm is the daily opening psalm (called the 'Invitatory') of the Church's Divine Office. It calls us to greater attention and devotion to God. ['Meribah' (which means 'dispute') and Massah ('temptation') are names given to the place where the Israelites, in the wilderness, grumbled because of lack of water and God enabled Moses to strike the rock with his staff to produce a flow of water (Ex 17:1-7).]

Second Reading   Colossians 3:1-5.9-11

In this final excerpt from Colossians, Paul encourages the Christians there to become Christ-like. Sharing in the death and resurrection of Christ through baptism gives us union with Christ, though this union has to be discovered gradually and will not be fully revealed until the *parousia* (the end times and the second coming of Christ to claim his faithful followers). We progress by avoiding all sinful behaviour. In the new creation, national, religious, racial and social distinctions will not exist.

Gospel   Luke 12:13-21

A request from the crowd that Jesus should intervene in a dispute about an inheritance gives Jesus the chance to condemn avarice as selfish and heartless (and to point out how foolish it can be).

Nineteenth Sunday in Ordinary Time • Year C

Collect

Since the Holy Spirit assures us that we are adopted children of God, we pray that we may learn how to live out that privilege and reach our inheritance of eternal life.

First Reading   Wisdom 18:6-9

The book of Wisdom was written in the first century BC in Alexandria to try to persuade Jews to remain faithful to their religion and values despite the attraction of hellenic culture popular at the time.

Today's extract recalls the time when God enabled the Jews to escape from slavery in Egypt, the events associated with that being proof that Israel was the chosen people of God. The people celebrated their covenant with God by the sacrifice of Passover, offered secretly, i.e., in their houses.

Psalm 32 (33)

Happy are the people the Lord has chosen as his own.

This hymn celebrates the providence and care with which God shows his love for his chosen people.

Second Reading   Hebrews 11:1-2.8-19

The next four Sundays will have extracts from the letter to the Hebrews, a document probably dating from around 67 AD, of an unknown author, written to Jews who, being persecuted for having become Christians, were showing signs of reverting to Judaism. There is great emphasis on comparing the Jewish priesthood with that of Jesus and on the superiority of the latter. The four extracts used in this year are from chapters 11 and 12.

Today's excerpt urges those addressed to remember that faith is concerned with things in the future which are to be hoped for but at present are unseen. It then illustrates this with several examples from Jewish history. The final sentence asserts that Isaac's 'death' was a parable of the death and resurrection of Christ and indeed of us all.

Gospel   Luke 12:32-48

Jesus teaches that our true and lasting home is with God. He therefore counsels us to be ready for the second coming of Christ, for judgment and the end of the world as we know it (all this is called the parousia). To Peter's question ("Is the parable for us or for everyone?"), scholars differ regarding Jesus' reply: either Jesus stresses its importance for the apostles (the stewards); or, assuming that Peter is asking about those invited to the banquet, Jesus ignores the question as unworthy.

Twentieth Sunday in Ordinary Time • Year C

Collect

We ask God, by his own love, to bring us to love him above everything else so that we may reach the inheritance with him that he has promised.

First Reading   Jeremiah 38:4-6.8-10

At the beginning of the sixth century BC, Jeremiah the prophet is imprisoned in Jerusalem and in fact is thrown into a dry cistern because he was preaching, as a message from God, that the people should surrender to the Chaldean besiegers and be taken into exile. Many are annoyed by this defeatist talk. However, before the prophet dies in the cistern, he is pulled out and set free.

Psalm 39 (40)

Lord, come to my aid!

The psalm is one of gratitude to God for his help in danger and distress and specifically and appropriately for a rescue 'from the deadly pit, from the miry clay'.

Second Reading   Hebrews 12:1-4

Following on from last week's passage, the letter to the Hebrews urges the Jewish converts to be taught by the examples from history of perseverance in faith and hope. Jesus himself endured the cross as well as the hostility of many; his example should encourage us to steadfast perseverance.

Gospel   Luke 12:49-53

This short passage collects several sayings of Jesus originally spoken on different occasions. 'Fire' means that which judges and separates out those destined for the kingdom. 'Baptism' here means the ordeal of the cross. The divisions within families indicate that Jesus does not settle for peace at any cost; hence there will be division between the eager and the contented, between those who seek conversion and the complacent.

Twenty-First Sunday in Ordinary Time
• Year C

Collect

We ask God to make us so obedient to him and so full of hope that, in this changing world, we may be intent on reaching the place of true happiness.

First Reading   Isaiah 66:18-21

This reading from the final chapter of Isaiah was probably written when the Jews had returned from exile in the second half of the sixth century BC. The meaning of the details is confusing. The passage looks forward to an eschatological age (a time at the end of the world as we know it) when (perhaps) Jews dispersed in many pagan nations and who worship God will be the means by which those nations will be converted and will come to Jerusalem to worship and serve God.

Psalm 116 (117)

> Go out to the whole world;
> proclaim the Good News.   or   Alleluia!

This short psalm is a summons to the whole world to worship the one true God.

Second Reading   Hebrews 12:5-7.11-13

The author of Hebrews reminds his readers that they are God's children and every father trains his children, sometimes with reprimands and punishment. Such means are, in fact, a sign of God's love and care for us.

Gospel   Luke 13:22-30

Luke informs us that, while making his way to Jerusalem, Jesus visited many places, teaching and preaching the establishment of God's kingdom. Entry to the kingdom when it is fulfilled in eternal life will neither be automatic nor easy. This leads to Jesus being more specific. Membership of God's chosen people does not ensure salvation. In fact, Jews may see many gentiles being saved while they, because of their sinfulness, are excluded from the kingdom.

Twenty-Second Sunday in Ordinary Time
• Year C

Collect

We ask God, from whom we receive everything good, to help us to love him more, to increase his gifts in us and to protect them with his care.

First Reading   Ecclesiasticus 3:17-20.28-29

Ecclesiasticus is a book by a Jewish scholar, Ben Sira (second century BC), anxious to repel the growing influence of pagan Greek ideas. Today's excerpt urges us to behave humbly, which both God and wise people prefer.

Psalm 67 (68)

In your goodness, O God,
you prepared a home for the poor.

This long psalm thanks God for all his protection and help at various stages in the history of the Jewish people. The extract used in today's Mass is not specific but praises God for his love of the lonely, the homeless, the captives and all who are in need.

Second Reading   Hebrews 12:18-19.22-24

This extract from Hebrews contrasts the spectacular display of God's majesty and power with which the first covenant (between God and his chosen people) was proclaimed in the desert (Exodus 19:12-20) and the circumstances in which the covenant of the New Law will be celebrated in eschatological times.

Gospel   Luke 14:1.7-14

Jesus has accepted an invitation to a meal with others in the house of a 'leading pharisee'. The main purpose of the advice to go to a low place at table is to emphasise that, in God's kingdom, God invites those who recognise their lowliness.

Then Jesus instructs the pharisee on those he should invite. We should not neglect those who cannot return the favour; our kindness and favours should be offered disinterestedly and not in expectation of something in return. Our conduct, therefore, should be modelled on God's treatment of us.

Twenty-Third Sunday in Ordinary Time
• Year C

Collect

We ask God to grant us, his adopted family, that, believing in Christ, we may be truly free and reach our promised inheritance.

First Reading   Wisdom 9:13-18

The book of Wisdom was written by a Jew in the 'hellenised' city of Alexandria and in the first century BC. It purports to be by King Solomon, famous for his wisdom. Today's reading is a reflection on our difficulty of discerning God's thinking and plans. Our material body impedes our thoughts and only God's gift of wisdom and the Holy Spirit enable us to have some inklings. (In the book of Wisdom, wisdom and spirit are the same and are seen as an attribute of God, personified for literary purposes.)

Psalm 89 (90)

O Lord, you have been our refuge
from one generation to the next.

The psalm is a meditation on the shortness of our life on earth and our need of wisdom to know this. This point is made in the midst of a general plea for God's help.

Second Reading   Philemon 9-10.12-17

Paul is probably in prison in Rome around 61 - 62 AD when he writes to Philemon, one of his converts in Colossae. The short and personal letter is about Onesimus, Philemon's slave, who had escaped. Onesimus has been converted by Paul who is now sending him back to Philemon. Paul recognises that legally Philemon still owns his slave but he begs him to treat Onesimus as a brother in Christ.

Gospel   Luke 14:25-33

Jesus continues his preaching – and attracting 'great crowds'. According to Luke, Jesus calls us to 'hate' our closest relatives but this is a Hebraism and an exaggeration for effect. (To reassure ourselves, see Matthew's report (10:37): 'Anyone who prefers . . .'. Moreover, Matthew does not include one's wife among the 'unpreferred', let alone among the 'hated'.) However, Jesus is demanding a total commitment to discipleship, and acceptance of hardship. The two parables show that we must be aware of the involvement needed as disciples, and not simply decide rashly on impulse.

Twenty-Fourth Sunday in Ordinary Time
• Year C

Collect

We ask God, our creator and ruler, to help us experience his mercy and willingly serve him.

First Reading   Exodus 32:7-11.13-14

The book of Exodus relates how, while Moses was with God on Mount Sinai and receiving the tablets with the Ten Commandments on them, the people had fallen into idolatry. God's fury and intention to punish his people are changed at the intense pleading of Moses.

Psalm 50 (51)

I will leave this place and go to my father.

This is the *Miserere*, the great psalm of repentance for sin. The sinner begs forgiveness for offences against God, asks God's graces for the future and, with humble contrition, seeks God's help to offer praise. The response anticipates today's gospel passage.

Second Reading   1 Timothy 1:12-17

The first of three readings from Paul's first letter to Timothy, whom he had left in charge of the church in Ephesus, on the west coast of Turkey (Asia Minor). In today's excerpt, Paul recalls with humble gratitude the mercy that God showed in calling him to faith and to preaching the word of God.

Gospel   Luke 15:1-32

The preaching of Jesus attracts tax collectors and sinners and this draws the contempt of pharisees (men who rigorously observed the religious and legal precepts of Judaism) and of scribes (official interpreters of Scripture, having authority in judicial decisions and entitled to membership of the Sanhedrin). Jesus responds with three parables to show God's desire to save each and every sinner who repents. Hence the parables of the lost sheep, the lost coin and the lost (or prodigal) son. In the last, the father is a symbol of God and his mercy; the elder son's resentment is like the attitude of some scribes and pharisees.

Twenty-Fifth Sunday in Ordinary Time • Year C

Collect

Since the basis of all God's commandments is love of him and of our neighbours, we ask for the grace to obey the commandments and so reach eternal life.

First Reading   Amos 8:4-7

God called Amos directly (and not from any prophetic confraternity) from his work as a shepherd. In mid-eighth century BC, Amos preached about the social injustice and corruption and hypocrisy rampant in city life. In this excerpt, he condemns dishonesty, especially among merchants. The day of the monthly new moon was, like the sabbath, a day of rest. The meaning of the phrase 'the pride of Jacob' is unclear – perhaps a term meaning the Lord.

Psalm 112 (113)

Praise the Lord, who raises the poor.   or   *Alleluia!*

This short psalm praises God and then, towards the end, thanks God for raising poor people from their misery.

Second Reading   1 Timothy 2:1-8

This excerpt contains advice for Timothy in Ephesus and, indeed, for us all. We should pray for everyone, especially our rulers. (Nero was the emperor when Paul was writing this letter.) He then makes the very important and clear statement: God our Saviour 'wants everyone to be saved'. Paul briefly expands this truth and adds that he has been chosen to be a herald and teacher of the faith 'to the pagans'.

Gospel   Luke 16:1-13

This gospel passage begins with the parable of the crafty steward, whom the master praises not for his dishonesty but for his astute foresight. Then follow several sayings of Jesus (perhaps at different times) on the right and wrong use of money. The first – 'use money. . .' – says that, if we are wealthy, our money should be used for good purposes (to be shared with the poor?) so that, after death, our beneficiaries (the poor?) will welcome us to heaven. The final two sentences at the end of the passage – 'No servant . . .' – are not relevant to the rest of today's gospel. They simply reiterate the total commitment that Jesus asks of his followers.

Twenty-Sixth Sunday in Ordinary Time
• Year C

Collect

Acknowledging God's infinite mercy, we pray for the grace to inherit his promises of eternal life.

First Reading   Amos 6:1.4-7

Again from the prophet Amos, who this time inveighs against the affluent who have no interest in anything but their own pleasure. The nation of Israel is on the road to disaster ('the ruin of Joseph') and the indolent wealthy will be the first to be carried off into exile.

Psalm 145 (146)

My soul, give praise to the Lord. or *Alleluia!*

This psalm praises the Lord for being a God who cares for the poor – the oppressed and imprisoned, the physically handicapped, the deprived and the neglected. It is part of morning prayer for Jews.

Second Reading   1 Timothy 6:11-16

Paul encourages Timothy to remember that he is dedicated to God's service and therefore must be a person of virtue and without faults so that he will gain eternal life at the second coming of Christ. The extract then develops this eschatological teaching about the end times, the parousia.

Gospel   Luke 16:19-31

The parable of the rich man and the beggar ('Lazarus' = 'God is my help') shows the contrast and gulf between rich and poor both in this life and in eternal life, but with an exact reversal of situations. The rich man is not shown as an exploiter, merely as one who is uninterested in others. The parable becomes personal when Jesus asserts that if his listeners (he was speaking to pharisees) pay no attention to Moses and the prophets, neither will they heed if someone rises from the dead.

Twenty-Seventh Sunday in Ordinary Time
• Year C

Collect

To God, whose kindness is far beyond our expectations, we pray for forgiveness and for the gifts that only he can know and bestow.

First Reading   Habakkuk 1:2-3; 2:2-4

Habakkuk wrote around 600 BC, anxious to discover why God, in punishing the people for their sinfulness, chooses the Chaldeans, who are even more evil than the Jews, to carry out this task of retribution. This is, in effect, the problem of evil. Habakkuk chooses, in this extract, to express the dilemma as a dialogue between himself and God, who responds to the prophet's complaint by telling him to be patient and await the eventual outcome.

Psalm 94 (95)

O that today you would listen to his voice!
Harden not your hearts.

The psalm thanks God and urges the people to show God proper reverence and attention, avoiding the ingratitude shown while in the wilderness.

Second Reading   2 Timothy 1:6-8.13-14

This is the first of four excerpts from Paul's second letter to Timothy. Paul reminds Timothy to seek renewal of the gift of the Spirit which he received when Paul imposed hands on him. Thus he will be bold in his preaching and patient in enduring hardships. He should be careful to ensure that his teaching is faithful to that which he was taught, for it is something of great value.

Gospel   Luke 17:5-10

When asked by the apostles to increase their faith, Jesus replies with an exaggeration in his reported response, to urge that it is in quality, not quantity, that faith should increase. Then he reminds them that, as servants of the Word, they are merely doing their duty when they faithfully carry out their work. They can never stop and rest, thinking that there is nothing further to do.

Twenty-Eighth Sunday in Ordinary Time
• Year C

Collect

We ask for God's grace to be always with us, urging us to help others.

First Reading   2 Kings 5:14-17

This episode is from the life of Elisha, successor of the prophet Elijah and active in mid-ninth century BC. Naaman, army commander in Aram (= Syria) has leprosy and, after having scoffed at the idea of going to Israel to bathe in the Jordan, agrees to do so and is cured. Naaman expresses faith in the God of the Jews and promises to worship no other god. Naaman's reason for requesting soil is because he is aware of the special relationship that God has with the soil and people of Israel; he therefore plans to build an altar to God in Damascus.

Psalm 97 (98)

The Lord has shown his salvation to the nations.

This psalm is an eschatological hymn with some emphasis on God as judge of the world. In the verses used today, God is acclaimed for the truth and love he has shown to Israel as well as for his salvation and justice to all nations.

Second Reading   2 Timothy 2:8-13

The second letter to Timothy is written from Rome where Paul is in prison. It is for his preaching of the risen Saviour that he suffers, and especially by his incarceration. Paul sums up his thoughts at that moment – resignation and faithfulness – by quoting some words from a Christian hymn.

Gospel   Luke 17:11-19

Jesus is going southwards in the Jordan valley, leaving Galilee and entering Samaria. Ten lepers are cured; only one, a Samaritan, returns to thank Jesus and to praise God.

Twenty-Ninth Sunday in Ordinary Time
• Year C

Collect
We ask God that we may always do his will and serve him sincerely.

First Reading   Exodus 17:8-13

From Exodus (the second book of the Pentateuch), we hear how, during their journey in the desert after their escape from Egypt, Joshua led the Israelites to victory in battle over the Amalekites, a nomadic tribe of the Negev. Military success depended on Moses keeping his arms raised, which he did with some ingenuity.

Psalm 120 (121)

Our help is in the name of the Lord
who made heaven and earth.

The psalm extols God as the constant guardian and protector of Israel.

Second Reading   2 Timothy 3:14-4:2

Paul reminds Timothy that he (Timothy) has known the Scriptures (i.e., the Old Testament) since he was young. Because Scripture is inspired by God, it gives wisdom and leads to salvation 'through faith in Jesus Christ'. Paul solemnly charges Timothy with the duty of proclaiming the Good News with perseverance and patience.

Gospel   Luke 18:1-8

This is a parable about a very independent judge and a dissatisfied widow, the latter through her persistence eventually overcoming the former's reluctance to attend to her pleas. Jesus uses the story to illustrate the need to keep praying and never give up. So, Jesus promises, God will always see justice done 'and done speedily'. In apparent contradiction, however, Jesus admits that sometimes there is a delay. Why is this so? To allow the guilty person time to repent and make retribution? To give an opportunity for human righting of the situation? Because God does not intervene directly until the parousia? Jesus gives no explanation. At the end, he wonders whether any of the necessary faith exists or will exist. The faith of which he speaks is a trust in God, relying no longer on our own resources but only on God's power.

Thirtieth Sunday in Ordinary Time • Year C

Collect

Asking God to increase our faith, hope and love, we also pray to be obedient to him so as to receive what he has promised.

First Reading   Ecclesiasticus 35:12-14.16-19

The book of Ecclesiasticus contains many items of good advice for the people, information about God and how to serve him etc. In this reading, the author is reassuring his readers of God's justice which does not allow him to show the slightest neglect in righting the wrongs suffered by the poor or the marginalised.

Psalm 33 (34)

This poor man called; the Lord heard him.

The psalm tells us of God's loving care for the unfortunate – the humble, the just, the broken-hearted, those spiritually crushed or captive.

Second Reading
2 Timothy 4:6-8.16-18

In this final extract from Paul's second letter to Timothy, the apostle speaks of his approaching death. (A libation is a drink-offering to God, poured over the victim in a Jewish sacrifice.) He looks forward with confidence to being in the presence of the visible Christ. He reports that, at a recent hearing of his case in court, he was without any human support; but the Lord came to his rescue (as Paul is sure he will continue to do before finally taking him to eternal life).

Gospel
Luke 18:9-14

The parable of the pharisee and the publican teaches us that God does not like a person who is proud of his virtue and boastful of his observance of the Law, and thus considers himself better than others. The person who is humble enough to know himself to be a sinner will receive God's mercy. Pharisees were convinced of their superiority, tax collectors aware of their ill-repute.

Thirty-First Sunday in Ordinary Time
• Year C

Collect

Recognising that even our service of God is his gift, we pray that we may proceed without mishap on the way to receive our promised inheritance.

First Reading
Wisdom 11:22-12:2

In this passage from the book of Wisdom, the relationship between God and the world is examined. God is infinitely greater, but is always merciful. He loves everything that exists, otherwise he would not have created it or continue conserving it. Although merciful, God wants his creatures to improve and so he gently admonishes and corrects them.

Psalm 144 (145)

I will bless your name for ever,
O God my King.

The four verses in today's psalm alternate between glorifying, praising and thanking God (first and third verses) and declaring our reasons – God is kind and compassionate to all, supportive and faithful (second and fourth verses).

Second Reading
2 Thessalonians 1:11-2:2

The first of three excerpts from Paul's second letter to the church in Thessalonika (north-east coast of Greece). The two letters to the Thessalonians are

Paul's first writings. He had been preaching in the city in AD 50 and the letters date from the years 50 and 51.

In today's passage he assures his converts of his prayers for them that they will continue growing in faith and love. He then tries to dampen their enthusiasm for an imminent second coming of Christ. Anticipation of an early parousia was current among the earliest Christians (see some chapters in the synoptics and even in Paul's letters) but here the apostle is cautious.

Gospel   Luke 19:1-10

Having reached Jericho on his way from Galilee to Jerusalem, Jesus invites himself to the house of Zacchaeus who, despite being a tax collector (and a senior one, so presumably heartily despised by all), had already shown his interest in Jesus. Zacchaeus experiences the grace of conversion (metanoia) which Jesus confirms; no one is excluded from salvation, no matter how apparently reprobate.

Thirty-Second Sunday in Ordinary Time
• Year C

Collect

We ask our divine Father to keep us free from all obstacles of mind or body that would hinder us from seeking the things of God.

First Reading   2 Maccabees 7:1-2.9-14

The books of the Maccabees cover the years 175 to 134 BC. They tell the story of the struggles of those Jews faithful to the religion and tradition of the people, trying to stem the increasing popularity of hellenism promoted by the Seleucid rulers of that era. The traditionalists were led by the family of Maccabees – Mattathias and his three sons, Judas, Jonathan and Simon. The second of the two books of the Maccabees is not a continuation of the first, but rather is in parallel with it; the second's aim is to impress and stimulate religiously and is less concerned with historical accuracy than the first book.

Today's excerpt from the second book is set during a persecution of the Jews by the Seleucid King Antiochus Epiphanes. It concerns seven brothers who, in the presence of their mother, refused to eat pig's flesh and were therefore martyred one after another. The reading gives some details of three of the deaths. In the words of the brothers, we have the first assertion of resurrection after death and then eternal life; and, since the Jews did not distinguish between soul and body, the assertion implies corporeal resurrection (although only explicitly of the virtuous in these texts).

Psalm 16 (17)

I shall be filled, when I awake,
with the sight of your glory, O Lord.

In this psalm, the innocent person trustingly pleads for God to 'hear a cause that is just'. The phrase 'when I awake' refers to awakening in the morning, although some like to think there may also be a reference to resurrection.

Second Reading   2 Thessalonians 2:16-3:5

Paul prays for the convert Christians whom he had taught at Thessalonika, asking God to give them comfort, strength and perseverance. He also asks their prayers for himself that the faith may spread rapidly and that it may not be damaged by people hostile to the message of salvation which Paul taught.

Gospel   Luke 20:27-38

Luke's Sunday gospels from the Thirteenth Sunday of Ordinary Time have been based on another source different from Mark. Here, Luke returns to Mark's earlier details about Jesus, though by no means copying then exactly.

The Sadducees' attempted reasoning to disprove or ridicule the teaching of Jesus on life after death is ignored by Jesus as fatuous and not requiring his attention. But he does assert the resurrection of the dead (when we shall live for ever and there will be no further need of marriage). Jesus also cites the text (Exodus 3:6) in which God calls himself the God of Abraham, Isaac and Jacob; even though these patriarchs are no longer living on earth, God continues to be their God – and so they are still alive.

Thirty-Third Sunday in Ordinary Time
• Year C

Collect

We ask 'the author of all that is good' to give us the happiness of being constant in our service of him.

First Reading   Malachi 3:19-20

The prophet Malachi was active probably at the start of the fifth century BC. He speaks, first, of the failure of both priests and people in their religious duties and, later, of the restoration of virtue. This latter is the subject of today's reading. The phrase 'sun of righteousness' is often taken to have a messianic reference.

Psalm 97 (98)

The Lord comes to rule the peoples with fairness.

A psalm that calls on all creation to acclaim the Lord. It has an eschatological dimension, looking forward to the time when God will come to rule the earth and all its peoples.

Second Reading   2 Thessalonians 3:7-12

In this last excerpt from 2nd Thessalonians, Paul states the general principle that his converts should imitate him. By doing so they will be imitating Jesus. He then goes on to a particular application of the principle. Idleness has to be avoided (and he has shown this by his own example). It is worse if idle people also interfere with others' working. He even goes so far as to recommend that people who refuse to work should not be allowed food.

Gospel   Luke 21:5-19

In the first of the three paragraphs of today's gospel, Jesus foretells the destruction of the temple and is asked by his disciples when that will happen. In the second, the response of Jesus mixes the times of two future events (as also in Mark 13:5-13): the destruction of the city and the temple by the Roman army (which in fact took place in AD 70) and (more explicitly) the end of the world when Jesus returns for the second coming and the judgment. The third paragraph also has dual application, but more explicitly to the events of AD 70. The terms used are biblical and apocalyptic and not necessarily to be taken literally. This 21st chapter, an account of the final days of Christ's public ministry, continues the eschatological theme (although not in the liturgy excerpts chosen) and, as for the date of the parousia, Jesus simply uses the parable of the ripening of the fig tree.

Our Lord Jesus Christ, King of the Universe • Year C

(Thirty-Fourth Sunday in Ordinary Time)

Collect

Since it is God's will that everything be restored in his Son, King of the Universe, we pray that all creation, freed from slavery, may always serve and praise God.

First Reading   2 Samuel 5:1-3

For a few years following the death of King Saul, the Israelites had been split into two nations, Israel (ten tribes) and Judah (the tribe of Judah, the previously absorbed tribe of Simeon and at least part of the tribe of Benjamin). This reading, from the second book of Samuel, recounts the occasion when Israel went to David, king of Judah, at his capital of Hebron and invited him to become king of a re-united Israel. The reunion was to last only until the death of Solomon, David's son.

Psalm 121 (122)

I rejoiced when I heard them say:
'Let us go to God's house.'

The pilgrims used to halt at the gates of Jerusalem and salute it with the cry of 'shalom!' ('peace!' - a gift; or a condition associated with hope for the messiah). In the city was God's house (the temple) and Jewish piety had great affection for holy Zion.

Second Reading   Colossians 1:12-20

In writing to the church in Colossae, Paul reminds the Christians (no longer only Jews) that God has made us citizens of his Son's kingdom and thereby we are redeemed and forgiven. There follows a hymn celebrating God's plan for his Son and, through him, for our salvation. The hymn may have been composed by Paul or merely quoted by him. It speaks of Christ as existing before any created things and of all creation being made 'through him and for him'. The phrase 'first-born of all creation' means not that Christ was created but that he has the first place of honour in creation. The Church is so closely related to Christ, sharing his life, that it can be called his body. Through his death and rising Christ brought peace and reconciliation to all creation, angels as well as humans.

Gospel   Luke 23:35-43

The scene is Calvary and Jesus dying on the cross. Those there, including leaders and soldiers, taunted Christ as claiming to be God's chosen one and a king, yet incapable of saving himself. One of the thieves joins in the insults, but the other, repentant and respectful and aware that Christ's kingdom was not of this world, begs Jesus' help when 'you come into your kingdom'.

The Collects and Readings for feasts
which can occur on Sundays

The Presentation of the Lord • 2 February

This feast was, until the reform of the liturgical calendar after Vatican II, known as the Purification of the Blessed Virgin Mary, although it was explained that Mary was not obliged to conform to the Jewish law since her motherhood 'was beyond ordinary laws'. The feast was also referred to as Candlemas Day because, before Mass, the priest blessed all the candles that would be needed for liturgical use that year. An example of the popularity of finding as much symbolism as possible in the liturgy in medieval times is the following from St Anselm: 'The wax of the candles signifies the virginal flesh of the Divine Infant, the wick his soul and the flame his divinity'.

Collect

On this feast of his Son's presentation in the temple, we pray that God may receive us into his presence with our minds made pure.

First Reading   Malachi 3:1-4

The prophet Malachi was writing around the middle of the fifth century BC at a time when priests and people in Israel had lost their religious zeal. The short reading today announces that, to purify and rekindle devotion, 'the Lord you are seeking will suddenly enter his Temple'. [The 'messenger' mentioned is sometimes identified with Elijah or John the Baptist (the new Elijah) while 'the angel of the covenant' is perhaps God himself or Jesus, the Son of God.]

Psalm 23 (24)

Who is the king of glory?
It is the Lord.

Today we use verses 7 to 10 which may refer to the occasion when the Ark of God's Covenant was, at King David's orders, brought up from the house of Obed-edom the Gath to a tent in the Citadel of David on Mount Sion in Jerusalem.

Second Reading   Hebrews 2:14-18

The letter to the Hebrews teaches that the Son of God became man to suffer, die and rise again in order to be the saviour of the human race. This passage assures us that Jesus was truly human so that he could fulfil this plan of God for our redemption.

Gospel   Luke 2:22-40

Our Lord's presentation in the temple is described in Luke's Gospel. The reading tells us that Mary and Joseph carefully observed all the requirements of the Jewish Law and that they made the offering that poor people made. We also read about Simeon, his prayer of thanksgiving to God (the canticle *Nunc dimittis* which speaks of God's salvation not only for Jews but also 'for all the nations' and 'a light to enlighten the pagans') and his words of prophecy to Mary; and we are told that Anna, a devout woman able to speak of God's plans, was present and subsequently told people about this child in terms of God's promise of a messiah.

[The *Nunc dimittis* is part of the official Night Prayer (Compline) of the Church.]

The Nativity of St John the Baptist • 24 June

John, the son of Zechariah and Elizabeth, preached a message of repentance in the wilderness of Judea and baptised at the Jordan nearby. His ministry was short because Herod Antipas, a son of Herod the Great and tetrarch of Galilee, had him imprisoned and beheaded. Herod Antipas' dislike and fear of John was largely due to the latter's denouncing him for repudiating his wife in order to enter an adulterous relationship with Herodias, the wife of his half-brother.

On the subject of the birth of John the Baptist, a pre-Vatican II Daily Missal tells us; 'After this feast the days become shorter while, on the contrary, after the Nativity of the Saviour, the days become longer. The Precursor must efface himself before Jesus, who is the true light of faith. "He must increase", says St John, "and I must decrease"'.

Collect

We ask God, who sent John the Baptist to prepare Israel for the coming of the messiah, to make us truly joyful and enable us to receive the divine gifts of salvation and peace.

First Reading   Isaiah 49:1-6

From Deutero-Isaiah, this is the second (of four) 'songs of the servant of the Lord'. It tells of a perfect disciple who proclaims the true faith, who suffers to atone for others' sins and, in the end, is exalted by God. Christians normally see this servant of God as the messiah, Jesus Christ. But in today's liturgy, it is John the Baptist to whom the passage refers.

Psalm 138 (139)

I thank you for the wonder of my being.

The psalm praises God's omniscience. The verses chosen concentrate on God's knowledge of and plan for a person (today's saint) before he was even conceived.

Second Reading   Acts 13:22-26

The passage is taken from an address that St Paul gave in the synagogue in the town of Antioch in Pisidia, in the interior of Asia Minor. This is Paul's first great discourse to a Jewish assembly. He said that, to keep his promise fully to King David, God raised up one of David's descendants, Jesus Christ, to be our Saviour. And, to herald the coming of Jesus, God sent John the Baptist.

Gospel   Luke 1:57-66.80

St Luke's Gospel (chapter 1) gives the account of the birth and naming of John the Baptist, son of Elizabeth and Zechariah. The latter had his power of speech restored and proclaims the canticle of thanksgiving and prophecy which we call the Benedictus. This is not included in today's Gospel Reading, but is recited daily at Lauds (Morning Prayer) in the Divine Office. The canticle contains many allusions to the Old Testament and especially to the Psalms.

Saints Peter and Paul, Apostles • 29 June

It is thought that both Peter and Paul were martyred in Rome during the persecution of the Emperor Nero, probably around the year 67 AD. The tradition is that Peter died by crucifixion (and it is said that, in humility, he asked to be crucified head downward) and Paul was beheaded. Last century during excavations under St Peter's Basilica, a tomb of the period was found, containing bones presumed to be of Peter. Paul's martyrdom is thought to have taken place at Tre Fontane, now a suburb of Rome not far from the present basilica of St Paul Outside the Walls.

Collect

We ask God that the Church may faithfully follow the teaching of the two apostles from whom we first received our faith.

First Reading   Acts 12:1-11

An account of Peter's miraculous escape from prison in which he was confined, awaiting trial. This happened between 41 and 44 AD, during a persecution of the Christians in Jerusalem by Herod Agrippa, a grandson of Herod the Great.

Psalm 33 (34)

From all my terrors the Lord set me free.   or

The angel of the Lord rescues those who revere him.

The psalm praises God's justice and gives thanks for his protection. The psalm is 'alphabetical', each verse beginning in sequence with the twenty-two letters of the Hebrew alphabet. We use the first eight, from *aleph* to *teth*.

Second Reading   2 Timothy 4:6-8.17-18

At the end of the second letter to Timothy, written in 65 AD, Paul recognises that his life on earth is almost over. He recalls God's goodness to him throughout his ministry and looks forward to being brought 'safely to the heavenly kingdom'.

Gospel   Matthew 16:13-19

Today's Gospel is the climactic moment in Christ's public ministry when he receives from Peter the great acknowledgement of his identity and, in turn, gives Peter (and, since the Church is to continue, his successors also) a position of primacy and authority among the disciples of Christ. All three synoptic Gospels report Peter's words: 'You are the Christ' (= the Messiah); only in Matthew's Gospel is Peter reported as adding 'the Son of the living God'. The word 'Peter' or 'Rock' had never been used as a person's name prior to this.

The use of the word 'church' (in Hebrew and Greek) is frequent in the Old Testament; basically, it means 'a summoned assembly' and, specifically, it meant 'the community of the chosen people'. Here it means 'the messianic community of Christ's followers' (who are those called into the kingdom of heaven (= of God), the keys of which are put in Peter's charge). Jesus builds the Church on Peter, who is a rock because of his faith in Christ, revealed to him by God.

The Transfiguration of the Lord • 6 August

The location of this event is uncertain. Some favour Mount Hermon in northern Galilee but most consider that Mount Tabor in the south of Galilee is the probable scene of the Transfiguration.

Collect

In the opening prayer today, our faith is confirmed by the presence at the transfiguration of two witnesses, Moses and Elijah, and our adoption as God's children is foreshadowed. We ask God that, hearing his Son's teaching and becoming his disciples, we may also have a share in his inheritance.

First Reading   Daniel 7:9-10.13-14

The Book of Daniel dates from 167-164 BC and is the last of the messianic prophecies of the Old Testament. It tells of the sufferings and success of Daniel and his three companions as captive exiles in Babylon in the sixth century BC and is meant as an encouragement to the Jews suffering persecution four centuries later.

In today's passage, written in apocalyptic genre, Daniel has a vision of God's final judgment of the human race, an event at which the saints are present. Then someone 'like a son of man' is presented to 'the Ancient of Days' and on him is conferred eternal kingship over all humanity.

For Christians, the vision had great messianic and eschatological significance. Especially notable is the term 'son of man' because Jesus applies it to himself. In Hebrew it is 'ben adam', which literally means a man; but here it clearly means a person who is, in some mysterious way, greater than the normal human.

Psalm 96 (97)

The Lord is king,
most high above all the earth.

The verses used today praise God, especially for his universal sovereignty, but they can also be applied to Christ and his triumphant work of salvation.

Second Reading   2 Peter 1:16-19

The second letter of Peter is an authoritative document, although the claim that the author is St Peter is doubtful (and hence the claim that the writer witnessed the transfiguration). The purpose of this passage is to reassure Christians that Christ would come again, the basis of this confidence being the transfiguration understood as a confirmation of prophecies of the second coming.

Gospel Year A: Matthew 17:1-9 • Year B: Mark 9:2-10 • Year C: Luke 9:28-36

Years A, B and C respectively use the Matthew, Mark and Luke versions. The narratives in Matthew and Mark are very similar; but Luke, although essentially agreeing with the other two, has a few variations of detail and therefore indicating that the evangelist used a different source. Moses and Elijah symbolise the Old Testament Law and prophets, and as it were, authenticating Jesus. He is the centre of the scene, in circumstances that point to his divinity. All three accounts report the important instruction from the Father: 'Listen to him'.

The Assumption of the Blessed Virgin Mary
• 15 August

Belief in the assumption of Mary (known in eastern churches as her dormition) is a very early tradition. The doctrine was solemnly defined by Pope Pius XII at St Peter's in Rome on 1st November during the Holy Year 1950. It states as a truth revealed by God that, at the end of her earthly life, Mary, the immaculate Mother of God, was taken, body and soul, to heaven. The location of the occurrence is not defined; Jerusalem and 'the House of Mary' near Ephesus in Turkey both claim the honour.

Collect

Acknowledging our belief that Mary was assumed, soul and body, to heaven, we ask God that we may be admitted to share the same eternal destiny.

First Reading   Apocalypse 11:19; 12:1-6.10

The book of Revelation or the Apocalypse was written towards the end of the first century AD, possibly by St John the Evangelist or by someone close to him. It is a book difficult to understand, due partly to its apocalyptic nature (visions, prophecies etc.) and partly to the apparently confused order of the contents.

The first reading today speaks of a pregnant woman and a dragon, and an attack by the latter on the woman, who flees to the safety of the desert while her child, now born, is taken straight to God and his throne. (Michael and the good angels defeat the dragon and his angels in battle and God's victory and Christ's authority are proclaimed.) The woman is thought, by many Christians, to represent Mary but the author more probably had in mind Israel as the mother of the messiah. There seem to be allusions to Moses and the Israelites' escape from Egypt and their years in the desert. The dragon is Satan and the stars dragged from the sky allude to the fallen angels allied to Satan.

Psalm 44 (45)

On your right stands the queen,
in garments of gold.

The psalm is a royal wedding song which may have been composed for the wedding of a king of Israel. Jewish religious tradition speaks of a wedding foretold between the messiah and Israel, while the Christian tradition regards the bride in this case as referring to Our Lady. (Ophir was in Arabia, on the coast of the Red Sea. Gold from Ophir was much esteemed.)

Second Reading   1 Corinthians 15:20-26

In the first letter to the Corinthians, chapter 15, Paul speaks of the risen Christ who has won resurrection from the dead for us all. This resurrection will take place, 'all of them in their proper order', and will be complete at the end of the world. There is no explicit reference to the fact of Mary's assumption.

Gospel   Luke 1:39-56

Luke tells the story of Mary's visit to her cousin Elizabeth, both of them pregnant. Although on other occasions when this gospel is used, the text of the Magnificat is omitted in the liturgy, it is included today. The canticle is recited daily in the Evening Prayer (Vespers) of the Church. It has some similarities to the messianic song of Hannah when she took her infant Samuel to the temple at Shiloh and left him in the care of Eli to be in the Lord's service for the rest of his life (I Samuel 2:1-10); but Hannah's song is much less personal than Mary's. The Magnificat has two important and more general ideas: that God favours the poor and powerless, and that, since Abraham, Israel has a special place in God's plans. Moreover, the faith of Mary shines forth throughout the prayer. In it, she is at one with her son's teaching and shows us how to follow him.

The Exaltation of the Holy Cross • 14 September

With the destruction of Jerusalem in AD 70, the consequent neglect of the site of Calvary and its deliberate concealment by the Emperor Hadrian at the start of the second century, nothing was known of the cross on which Jesus died. It is said that Helena, mother of the Emperor Constantine, on pilgrimage in the Holy Land, found the cross on this date (perhaps c.330) and its authenticity was confirmed by miraculous signs. On the same date, 14th September, in 335, the basilica, built at the orders of Constantine and enclosing both Calvary and the Holy Sepulchre, was dedicated.

Collect

Since it is God's will that we should be saved through his Son's death on the cross, we pray that, knowing of this on earth, we may also receive the grace of its effect, eternal life.

First Reading   Numbers 21:4-9

This reading is from the book of Numbers and recounts an incident that occurred as the Israelites travelled through the desert from slavery in Egypt to the land God had promised them. The Israelites became rebellious because of the harsh conditions of life in the wilderness and wanted to return to Egypt. God punished their attempt at revolt by sending a plague of serpents from whose bites many died. The people realised their sin and begged Moses to ask God to end the punishment. Moses was told by God to make a bronze serpent and thereafter anyone bitten by a serpent looked at the bronze serpent and was saved from death. This incident is seen by Christians as a sign of the future Saviour of mankind, raised on the cross.

Psalm 77 (78)

Never forget the deeds of the Lord.

This long psalm, from which we read vv. 1-2 and 34-38, is a reflection on the history of the Israelites. It speaks of God's special care for them, their infidelity to this covenant of love, and God's willingness to forgive them.

Second Reading

Philippians 2:6-11

The extract from St Paul's letter to the Philippians is an early Christian hymn, written or quoted by the apostle, in which we acknowledge Christ's twofold humbling of himself (incarnation and crucifixion) for our salvation and God's response so that the whole universe would acclaim him with the divine name of Lord.

Gospel

John 3:13-17

In John's Gospel, chapter 3, Jesus reveals to Nicodemus ('a leading Jew') that God sent his only Son into the world to save the world. Specifically, Jesus explains that, just as the bronze serpent was lifted up in the desert and those who looked on it were saved (first reading), so 'the Son of Man' will also be lifted up so that those who believe in him will be given eternal life.

[In John's Gospel, Christ's being raised on the cross for our salvation is part of his 'exaltation'. The greatness of the cross is not to make us glory in suffering as such, but to discover the liberating power of divine love when experienced in all its depth.]

The Solemnity of All Saints • 1 November

In Rome, the Pantheon had been built (end of first century BC) and then rebuilt (beginning of second century AD) as a temple to all the pagan gods. Early in the seventh century, the pope transferred from the catacombs to the Pantheon the remains of many martyrs and the temple was dedicated as a Christian basilica in 610. It is from this that the present feast originates.

Collect

We pray that we may be fully reconciled with God, seeking the intercession of all the saints whose memory we celebrate and venerate today.

First Reading

Apocalypse 7:2-4.9-14

In the Apocalypse, the author narrates a vision he had in which a huge number of saints are given their eternal reward in the presence of God and the Lamb, whom they acclaim and honour. The opening of the reading refers to twelve thousand from each of the twelve tribes of Israel; the conclusion of the passage refers to the martyred victims of persecution (probably meaning that of Nero, 64 - 67 AD).

Psalm 23 (24)

Such are the men who seek your face, O Lord.

This psalm praises God and recognises those who love and obey him.

Second Reading   1 John 3:1-3

The first letter of John is addressed to the Christians of Asia Minor whose unity is threatened by early heresies. In the extract read, St John speaks of God's loving care of us as his adopted children. Eternal life awaits us if we live good lives on earth.

Gospel   Matthew 5:1-12

The teaching of Jesus on the beatitudes, the first part of the Sermon on the Mount, is chosen for this feast of All Saints. Our Lord's teaching on the beatitudes introduces a moral revolution and the reform of existing moral values not only of the Jewish world but also of the then prevalent Roman-Hellenistic culture. The general principles of the eight beatitudes are exemplified by the subsequent parts of the Sermon on the Mount (as Matthew arranges Christ's teaching) and throughout the rest of this Gospel.

The Dedication of the Lateran Basilica
• 9 November

The Lateran palace was a gift from the newly Christian Emperor Constantine to the pope, early in the fourth century. The palace became the papal residence and the church, built alongside, became the cathedral church of the diocese of Rome (as it still is). Consequently, it is called 'Omnium urbis et orbis ecclesiarum mater et caput'. Its full title is the Basilica of Our Saviour, St John the Baptist and St John the Evangelist; but it is commonly known as St John Lateran.

Collect

Recognising that God chooses living stones with whom to build for himself a Church on earth, we ask that he confer even greater gifts to his people so that they may also be building and adorning the Church in heaven.

First Reading   Ezekiel 47:1-2.8-9.12

Ezekiel was writing at the end of the sixth century BC for the Jews exiled in Babylon. The final chapters, including this one, look forward to their return to Israel and make preparations for it. This reading is a vision of the temple in Jerusalem to be rebuilt, with water flowing from it in abundance to make the district fertile, especially eastwards towards the Jordan Valley and the Dead Sea ('to the Arabah and to the sea', chapter 47:8).

Psalm 45 (46)

The waters of a river give joy to God's city,
the holy place where the Most High dwells.

This psalm speaks of God's presence in the temple guarding the Holy City while (symbolically) waters purify and fertilise the land.

Second Reading   1 Corinthians 3:9-11.16-17

In his first letter to the Christians in Corinth, Paul tells them they are God's sacred temple, whose foundation is Christ and in which the Holy Spirit dwells.

Gospel   John 2:13-22

St John tells us of the occasion when Jesus was in Jerusalem and, while there for the feast of Passover, he rid the temple of those defiling the sacred building by buying and selling. To the protests that followed, Jesus perplexes and confuses those objecting that he has no right to act in that way with this rejoinder: 'if this sanctuary is destroyed, I shall rebuild it in three days'. The use of words with double meanings (whose sense his followers understand later) is found now and again in the fourth Gospel. When celebrating the feast of the dedication of a particular church, we remember that, as well as Jesus referring to his body as a temple or sanctuary, we also speak of the Church as built of living stones.

The Immaculate Conception of the Blessed Virgin Mary • 8 December

From the early centuries of the second Christian millennium, belief in, and devotion to, the immaculate conception of the Blessed Virgin gradually spread in the Church. Blessed John Duns Scotus was a prominent proponent of the doctrine. Its justification is summed up in three words: potuit, decuit, ergo fecit *('it was possible, it was fitting, therefore it was done'). On this day in 1854, Pius IX officially proclaimed the doctrine as a dogma of the Church.*

Collect

We pray to God, who preserved Mary from even original sin by the foreseen redeeming death of his Son and so made her a fitting human mother for the same Son; our petition is that, through her prayers, we may be freed from sin and be made fit to be in God's presence.

First Reading Genesis 3:9-15.20

The book of Genesis tells the story of Adam and Eve's disobedience, the original sin which is transmitted to their descendants, to all human beings, except Mary. The serpent is a disguise for the devil whom God's words show to be the constant enemy of humankind. In God's words, a hint of his plan for our ultimate salvation is given so that the words are sometimes called the proto-evangelium. The identity of the pronoun 'it' in the phrase 'it will crush your head' is a matter of conjecture. The Hebrew text has a neuter singular pronoun; the Greek has a masculine pronoun, leading to a messianic interpretation; the Latin has the feminine form and so is applied to Mary, as mother of the messiah.

Psalm 97 (98)

Sing a new song to the Lord
for he has worked wonders.

The psalm is a hymn praising God as the loving saviour of all things. Its final verse (not used in today's liturgy) speaks of God judging the earth so the pssalm is regarded as eschatological.

Second Reading Ephesians 1:3-6.11-12

In the first chapter of the letter to the Ephesians, St Paul explains, and gives thanks for, God's eternal plan for us. The plan involves several graces, unearned by us but awarded through the merits of Christ (and which will not be fully granted until we reach the next life). The implication, of course, is that Christ saves us from our sins (and for Mary, there was anticipated redemption from original sin).

Gospel Luke 1:26-38

St Luke's Gospel tells the story of the annunciation and therefore of the human conception of God's Son in the womb of Mary who, in preparation for this moment, had herself been conceived immaculate in the womb of her own mother.